The School Years

companion volumes

The Early Years
Assessing and Promoting Resilience in Vulnerable Children 1
Brigid Daniel and Sally Wassell
ISBN 1 84310 013 4

Adolescence
Assessing and Promoting Resilience in Vulnerable Children 3
Brigid Daniel and Sally Wassell
ISBN 1 84310 019 3

Set of three workbooks
ISBN 1 84310 045 2

of related interest

Child Development for Child Care and Protection Workers
Brigid Daniel, Sally Wassell and Robbie Gilligan
ISBN 1 85302 633 6

The Child's World
Assessing Children in Need
Edited by Jan Horwath
ISBN 1 85302 957 2

Approaches to Needs Assessment in Children's Services
Edited by Harriet Ward and Wendy Rose
ISBN 1 85302 780 4

Social Work with Children and Families
Getting into Practice
Ian Butler and Gwenda Roberts
ISBN 1 85302 365 5

Creating a Safe Place
Helping Children and Families Recover from Child Sexual Abuse
NCH Children and Families Project
ISBN 1 84310 099 6

The School Years

Assessing and Promoting Resilience in Vulnerable Children 2

Brigid Daniel and Sally Wassell
Illustrated by Iain Campbell

Jessica Kingsley Publishers
London and Philadelphia

The right of Brigid Daniel and Sally Wassell to be identified as authors of this work has been asserted by them in accordance with the Copyright, Designs and Patents Act 1988.

First published in the United Kingdom in 2002
by Jessica Kingsley Publishers Ltd
116 Pentonville Road
London N1 9JB, England
and
325 Chestnut Street
Philadelphia, PA 19106, USA

www.jkp.com

Copyright © 2002 Brigid Daniel and Sally Wassell

Illustrations © 2002 Iain Campbell

Library of Congress Cataloging in Publication Data

A CIP catalog record for this book is available from the Library of Congress

British Library Cataloguing in Publication Data

A CIP catalogue record for this book is available from the British Library

ISBN 1 84310 018 5

Printed and Bound in Great Britain by
Athenaeum Press, Gateshead, Tyne and Wear

Contents

Acknowledgements

The writing and production of these workbooks was financially supported by the Social Work Services Inspectorate of the Scottish Executive. We would like to thank practitioners who helped to develop the material in these workbooks from Perth Social Work Department, Maryhill Social Work Centre, Glasgow and Children's Centres in North Edinburgh. We would also like to thank Robbie Gilligan, Professor of Social Work and Social Policy, and Director, Children's Research Centre, Trinity College, Dublin, and Jim Ennis, Elaine Ennis and Amelia Wilson of the Centre for Child Care and Protection Studies, Department of Social Work, University of Dundee for conceptual development and Helen Wosu for detailed comments. We are also extremely grateful to Stacey Farmer for administrative support. Thanks also to Christine Henderson and David Willshaw for support and encouragement.

Some of the issues in the workbooks have previously been published in Daniel, B., Wassell, S. and Gilligan, R. (1999) '"It's just common sense isn't it?": Exploring ways of putting the theory of resilience into action.' *Adoption and Fostering 23*, 3, 6–15 and are reproduced with the permission of British Agencies for Adoption and Fostering (BAAF). The Index of Empathy has been reproduced with the permission of the author and the Society for Research in Child Development. The table of Kohlberg's stages of moral development has been reproduced from Schaffer, H.R. (1996) *Social Development* with the permission of Blackwell Publishers Inc.

1
Introduction to Resilience

Ecological framework

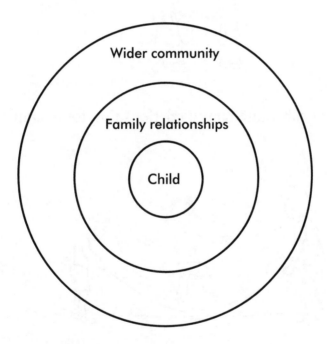

Figure 1.1 Three ecological levels at which resilience factors can be located

Throughout these workbooks the practitioner is encouraged to place assessment and intervention practice within an ecological framework (Bronfenbrenner 1989). This entails considering what resources might be available to the child at each of three levels (see Figure 1.1):

1. the individual, for example, in dispositional and temperamental attributes

2. close family or substitute family relationships, for example, in secure attachments

3. the wider community, for example, in extrafamilial supports.

All the checklists will address aspects of each of these levels and suggestions for intervention will be provided for different ecological levels.

Resilience

Resilience can be defined as: 'Normal development under difficult conditions' (Fonagy *et al.* 1994).

Due to a wide range of practice and theoretical research, the protective factors that support positive outcomes, despite adversity, are becoming better understood (Rutter

1985; Werner 1990; Werner and Smith 1992). These protective factors that are associated with long-term social and emotional well-being have been located at all levels of the child's ecological social environment. The existence of protective factors can help explain why one child may cope better with adverse life events than another. The level of individual resilience can be seen as falling on a dimension of resilience and vulnerability (see Figure 1.2).

Figure 1.2 Dimension on which individual resilience can be located

This dimension is usually used to refer to intrinsic qualities of an individual. Some children are more intrinsically resilient than others because of a whole range of factors that will be detailed later (Werner and Smith 1992). For example, an 'easy' temperament is associated with resilience in infancy.

A further dimension for the understanding of individual differences is that of protective and adverse environments; this dimension covers extrinsic factors and is therefore located at the outer ecological levels of family and wider community. Examples of protective factors are the existence of a close attachment and the presence of a supportive extended family member (see Figure 1.3).

Figure 1.3 Dimension on which factors of resilience around the child can be located

When considered together these dimensions provide a framework for the assessment of adverse and positive factors at all ecological levels of a child's socio-emotional environment (Daniel, Wassell and Gilligan 1999) (see Figure 1.4).

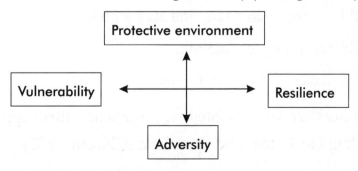

Figure 1.4 Framework for the assessment of resilience factors

The two dimensions will interact, an increase in protective factors will help to boost a child's individual resilience. Therefore, the workbook encourages the assessment of potential protective factors at each ecological level, with the aim of building up protective factors and thus boosting resilience.

Resilience is a complex issue and some caution is required. For example, it can be possible for children to appear to be coping well with adversity, whereas in fact they may be internalising their symptoms (Luthar 1991). Apparent coping cannot be taken at face value and careful, wide-ranging assessment is essential.

The assessment of resilience is not straightforward: the vast majority of studies have been carried out retrospectively. However, a number of checklists have been devised that aim to measure levels of resilience. For example, the International Resilience Project uses a simple checklist of 15 items that indicate resilience in a child (Grotberg 1997, p.20):

1. The child has someone who loves him/her totally (unconditionally).

2. The child has an older person outside the home she/he can tell about problems and feelings.

3. The child is praised for doing things on his/her own.

4. The child can count on her/his family being there when needed.

5. The child knows someone he/she wants to be like.

6. The child believes things will turn out all right.

7. The child does endearing things that make people like her/him.

8. The child believes in power greater than seen.

9. The child is willing to try new things.

10. The child likes to achieve in what he/she does.

11. The child feels that what she/he does makes a difference in how things come out.

12. The child likes himself/herself.

13. The child can focus on a task and stay with it.

14. The child has a sense of humour.

15. The child makes plans to do things.

Although many factors can be associated with resilience, there appear to be three fundamental building blocks that underpin them (Gilligan 1997):

1. A secure base, whereby the child feels a sense of belonging and security.

2. Good self-esteem, that is, an internal sense of worth and competence.

3. A sense of self-efficacy, that is, a sense of mastery and control, along with an accurate understanding of personal strengths and limitations.

These workbooks cover six domains of a child's life that will contribute to each of these three building blocks of resilience.

Because resilience is associated with better long-term outcomes, it can be used as a guiding principle when planning for children whose lives have been disrupted by abuse and or neglect and who may require to be looked after away from home (Gilligan 1997). Indeed:

> Resilience – the capacity to transcend adversity – may be seen as the essential quality which care planning and provision should seek to stimulate as a key outcome of the care offered. (Gilligan 1997, p.14)

When the home life of a child is disrupted for whatever reason, considerable attention is rightly paid to the issue of attachment and to placement, either in supporting the child to live at home or in the provision of an appropriate alternative home life. However, whatever the arrangements for the day-to-day care of such children, attention can also be paid to fostering their resilience. This approach recognises that although it may not always be possible to protect children from further adversity, and that while it may not always be possible to provide an ideal environment for them, boosting their resilience should enhance the likelihood of a better long-term outcome.

A resilience-based approach focuses on maximising the likelihood of a better outcome for children by building a protective network around them. The concept of resilience increasingly offers an alternative framework for intervention, the focus being on the assessment of potential areas of strength within the child's whole system. As yet, there is very little research into proactive attempts to promote resilience.

Whatever arrangements are made for the care of the child, this approach offers social workers a real focus for positive practice. This approach enables a move away from an assumption that a parent or alternative placement will provide all that the child needs. Instead the emphasis is on building a network of support from the resources available, and adding to them with professional support where necessary. It also emphasises the importance of building on the potential areas of resilience within the child or young person, for example, by maximising opportunities for engaging in hobbies, associating with friends, experiencing success, making a contribution and so on. What is important is that practitioners have the theoretical grounding that assures them that they can make a difference to the outcomes for children with such measures, even if they never see the results themselves. This assurance should help to reduce feelings of powerlessness and purposelessness.

DOMAINS OF RESILIENCE

Throughout the workbooks aspects of resilience in six domains will be considered (see Figure 1.5).

Figure 1.5 Six domains of resilience

Factors within each of these domains of a child's life, at each of the three ecological levels, are known to contribute to a child's level of vulnerability or resilience to adversity such as abuse, neglect and loss. More detail will be provided about each domain in the relevant section below.

It will be noted that these domains are similar to, but not identical with, the dimensions used in the Looking After Children (LAC) materials (Parker *et al.* 1991). However, much of the information required to assess resilience will be contained in completed LAC materials. The seven LAC dimensions can be linked with the six domains of resilience as follows:

1. Health: secure base

2. Education: education

3. Emotional and behavioural development: secure base/friendships/positive values

4. Family and peer relationships: secure base/friendships

5. Self-care and competence: secure base/social competencies

6. Identity: talents and interests

7. Social presentation: social competencies.

SUMMARY OF FACTORS ASSOCIATED WITH RESILIENCE DURING SCHOOL YEARS

Individual factors associated with resilience

- female

- sense of competence and self-efficacy

- internal locus of control

- empathy with others

- problem-solving skills

- communication skills

- sociable

- independent

- reflective, not impulsive

- ability to concentrate on schoolwork

- autonomy (girls)

- emotional expressiveness (boys)

- sense of humour

- hobbies

- willingness and capacity to plan.

Family factors associated with resilience

- close bond with at least one person

- nurturance and trust

- lack of separations

- lack of parental mental health or addiction problems

- required helpfulness

- encouragement for autonomy (girls)

- encouragement for expression of feelings (boys)

- close grandparents

- family harmony

- sibling attachment

- four or fewer children

- sufficient financial and material resources.

Wider community factors associated with resilience

- neighbour and other non-kin support

- peer contact

- good school experiences

- positive adult role models.

2

When and How to Use the Workbook

When?

These workbooks are intended as an aid to planning purposeful intervention with children and young people (see Figure 2.1). They are to be used in conjunction with Looking After Children materials when carrying out a comprehensive assessment of

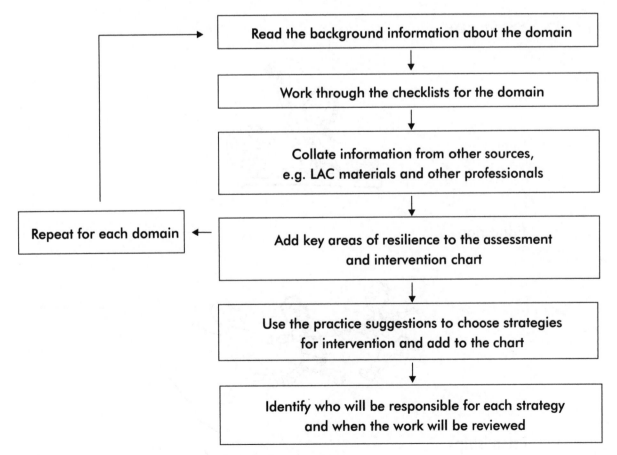

Figure 2.1 Process of assessment and planning for intervention

need; they can also be used to provide a baseline assessment against which the efficacy of intervention can be evaluated. They can be used to aid planning for children and young people living at home and for those living away from home.

How?

Ensure that you have chosen the appropriate workbook from one of three:

1. Pre-school children (early years)

2. School-age children

3. Adolescents.

The workbook takes you through a process of assessment for each of the six domains:

1. Secure base

2. Education

3. Friendships

4.   Talents and interests

5.   Positive values

6.   Social competencies.

Child checklist

When using the child's checklist try, as much as possible, to involve the child directly in the process. Explain what you are trying to find out and cover each of the points in the checklists with the child. Reword as appropriate. Try to arrange as much direct observation of behaviour as possible.

Parent/carer checklist

Go through the parent/carer checklist with any significant parent or carer. If there are significant differences between different people's responses, then explore this with the respondents and aim to reach a consensus on areas to work on.

A decision will need to be made for each situation as to whether to concentrate on an assessment of parental environment or carer environment. When the aim is for the child to stay at or return home, the focus may need to be upon home environment. If the child is to be accommodated on a long-term basis away from home, then the focus may need to be upon assessment of carer environment with a view to looking for aspects that might help with boosting resilience.

Use the checklists as a guide only, gather information from as wide a range of sources as possible, particularly from the LAC materials, and try to involve the child as much as possible, taking account of age and stage of development.

Assessment

Once you have assessed a domain, identify areas of actual or potential resilience at any ecological level that could be targeted for intervention and note them on the assessment and intervention chart. The assessment process is completed by bringing the information from each of the six domains together onto the chart.

Intervention

The workbook then takes you through a process of planning intervention. Look through the intervention strategies for each domain and use them to help plan strategies for the targeted areas for intervention. Note the strategies onto the assessment and intervention chart. In consultation with key people in the child's life, identify who will be responsible for each strategy. Remember to consider the informal network as well as professionals.

Evaluation

Ensure that a plan for evaluation and ongoing monitoring is built into the strategy for intervention and note this onto the assessment and intervention chart.

Please remember:

1. One social worker cannot do it all. Aim to develop a network of formal and informal supports around the child or young person.

2. Look at existing, mainstream community resources.

3. Try to balance intervention that aims to build on existing strengths, with strategies for boosting less strong areas.

4. Positive effects in one domain can spill over to another, the domains should therefore not be viewed as independent and separate, but as interactive and dynamic.

Assessment and intervention chart

Domain	What areas of resilience, at any ecological level, will we target now?	How will we do this?	Who will be responsible for this?	How and when will we measure progress?
Secure base				
Education				

✓

Friendships			
Talents and interests			
Positive values			
Social competencies			

Part I

Assessment

3

Secure Base

Background information

There is a clear association between the presence of a secure attachment relationship and resilience in the face of adversity (Werner 1990). The importance of attachment ties has been recognised in child-care practice for many years and normally underpins planning (Daniel *et al.* 1999; Fahlberg 1991; Howe 1995; Howe *et al.* 1999). It is during early years that the foundations of attachment are laid down. The classic studies to demonstrate attachment behaviour are normally carried out with toddlers, but elements of the behaviour can also be observed in older children (Ainsworth *et al.* 1978). These studies have shown that attachment behaviours can fall into one of several distinctive patterns. The most important distinction is between *secure* and *insecure* attachment. Young children who are classified as showing *secure* attachment play happily when their care-giver is present, protest when they leave and go to them for comfort on their return. They will show some wariness of strangers and choose their care-giver for comfort when upset or fearful. What they have is a base that not only is stable, but also acts as a springboard to the wider social world. Long-term resilience is associated with the opportunity to develop a secure attachment to at least one person.

Children who are classified as *insecure* may show one of four patterns.

1. If *avoidant* they tend to shun the care-giver after a separation and appear not to discriminate markedly in their behaviour towards a stranger and their care-giver.

2.	If *ambivalent* they appear to want comfort from the care-giver after a separation, but at the same time show resistance to comfort, for example by squirming out of a hug.

3.	A further form of insecure attachment, known as *disorganised*, is demonstrated in a mixture of reactions where the child appears confused and unable to feel comforted by the care-giver. Children who have been abused or neglected are more likely to show insecure patterns of attachment.

4.	Another pattern of insecure attachment has been identified by Downes (1992) that is characterised by an *anxious preoccupation* with the availability of the carer. It is a pattern that can often be encountered in practice with abused and neglected children.

School-aged children may not show such overt signs of attachment, but their need for a secure base is as great as is the young child's. Children who are securely attached are more likely to be able to make the separation needed to attend school, they are more likely to make good relationships with peers at school and their concentration is likely to be better.

Secure attachment is associated with a parenting style that is warm and sensitive. The parent has to be able to take account of the child's needs and temperament and respond appropriately. Patterns of attachment are, therefore, the products of a *relationship* between the child and the adult, and are influenced by the interaction between the child (with his or her temperament) and the adult. The early pattern of attachment acts as a kind of template or internal working model for later relationships. The internal working model is, therefore, based upon the child's sense of self and his or her experience of others. Howe *et al.* (1999, p.25) summarise it in the following way:

Self (loved, effective, autonomous and competent) + other people (available, cooperative and dependable) = *secure* attachment patterns.

Self (unloved but self-reliant) + other people (rejecting and intrusive) = *avoidant* attachment patterns.

Self (low value, ineffective and dependent) + other people (neglecting, insensitive, unpredictable and unreliable) + *ambivalent* attachment patterns.

Self (confused and bad) + other people (frightening and unavailable) = *disorganised* attachment patterns.

An important factor in the attachment relationship is the parent's own attachment history and the meaning it has for him or her. The way that adults talk about their own attachment experiences provides insight into their own level of security. Adults whose experience was of an abusive or neglectful childhood need not themselves be insecure. They can be considered secure if they have had an opportunity to process their experiences and can recount those experiences in a coherent way that suggests that they can make sense of their past (Main and Weston 1981). Having the opportunity and ability to reflect upon attachment experiences is key to overcoming difficult or disturbing past circumstances (Fonagy *et al.* 1994). It is also important to consider the ways in which current circumstances might undermine parents' ability to be sensitive to their child's needs, such as a difficult relationship with a partner, poverty, poor housing, social isolation and so on.

Children may have a secure relationship with one person (for example, the father) and insecure with another (for example, the mother), therefore the quality of all important relationships must be assessed (Fox, Kimmerly and Schafer 1991). The aim in practice is to ensure that children are provided with a secure base, either by improving the relationship with the parent/s or, if necessary, by finding an alternative attachment figure. Sometimes it can take a while to find long-term carers who will provide such secure relationships, but in the mean time there is tremendous potential for what Brooks (1994) describes as 'charismatic' adults to have a direct influence on a child's developing understanding of relationships. Insecure internal working models of attachment can change in the context of the formation of new, more secure relationships (Feeney and Noller 1996). During school years children will encounter a range of other adults, and among them may find someone that they can develop a relationship with. In practice, therefore, the aim would be to capitalise on the potential offered by any people, including absent fathers, siblings and extended family, family friends or professional staff, who take an interest in the child . Resilience theory would suggest an emphasis on building a protective network of support from all the resources available, and adding to them with professional support where necessary.

✓

SECURE BASE CHECKLIST
CHILD

In a thorough and comprehensive text, Howe *et al.* (1999) set out detailed guidance for the assessment of patterns of attachment and the planning of intervention. If initial assessment suggests attachment problems to be the key issue then we would recommend that you consult this book for more information. They suggest that assessment must include making inquiries of the files and the wider professional network, observing children in various circumstances, and interviewing parents and children.

There needs to be a decision about which attachment relationships to assess. It is recommended that if the child is living at home then an assessment be carried out on all significant adults, whether resident in the house or not, for example, mother, father, grandparent. If the child is living away from home then the relationship with the carer or keyworker should be assessed, as well as any continuing family relationships. The following checklists should therefore be used flexibly and be adjusted according to requirements.

Does this child appear to feel secure?

1. Observe the child in a range of settings, at home and school. Look at how he or she deals with stress and distress, at how he or she relates to adults and other children and at how willing the child is to explore the environment. From such observations it should be possible to build up a picture of the child's general level of security. Teachers' views will be very helpful here, as they are, of course, able to observe the child all day, in a range of situations.

Ask the child:

1. Who do you think is the person in your life who most cares about you and loves you?

2. Who is important in your life now?

3. Who do you see?

4. Who would you like to see?

5. Who are you closest to?

6. Is there anyone you are not seeing you would like to see?

7. Is there someone who used to look after you/live with you/spend time with you who you don't see now but would like to see again?

8. How often do you see important people you do not live with? Is this too little, too often, about right?

9. Is there anything that you would like to change about who you see?

10. Who helps you if you have a problem?

11. How do they know that you might need some help?

12. Who is most pleased when things go well for you?

13. Who can you talk to if you want something in your life to change?

14. When you say goodbye to someone you are close to, say, when you go to school, how does it make you feel?

15. Can you describe any separations or losses that you remember happening?

Does the current parent or carer environment provide the child with a secure base?

1. Observe the interaction between the child and each significant adult. Use the observations of the verbal and non-verbal aspects of the relationship and the consistency and sensitivity of the adult's response to the child to gauge the quality of the attachment relationship.

2. Observe the child at times of separation from, and reunion with, significant adults. Does the child show a healthy pattern of separation or are there signs of over-anxiety, clinginess or indifference?

Ask the child:

1. What are the routines in your house for mealtimes, bedtimes and so on?

2. If you are upset about something, how do you show what you feel and who would you turn to?

3. Do you feel that your parent or carer is able to make time for you?

4. (If the child is living away from home) do you have contact with a parent and do you know why you have that contact?

What are the wider resources that contribute to the child's attachment network?

In collaboration draw an ecomap using circles to represent the child and any other person who is, or who has been, important to the child, including other children. Map the child's network, with the person who is most important to the child closest to him or her. A series of ecomaps can be used to represent the past, the present and what the child would like for the future.

Ask the child:

1. Is there any person in your family, wider family, or among other people that you know, who you think you would like to spend more time with?

2. Do you attend any clubs or activities run by adults that you like and trust? If not, would you like to attend something like this?

SECURE BASE CHECKLIST
PARENT/CARER

Does this child appear to feel secure?

Ask the parent/carer:

1.   Who is important to this child?

2.   How does the child communicate this?

3.   Is there someone the child misses and doesn't see?

4.   Is there someone who used to be involved with this child but who they no longer see?

5.   What changes might/does this child wish to see in their relationships?

6.   What does he or she do if upset? How does he or she show their distress and show that they want comfort?

7.   How willing is he or she to explore new places, activities and so on?

8.   Does he or she react differently to unknown adults from how he or she reacts to known adults?

9.   What significant losses or separations has this child experienced?

Does the current parent or carer environment provide the child with a secure base?

1.   Ask the parent about his or her own experiences of loss, separation and rejection, experiences of emotional upsets, hurts and sickness and his or her experiences of love and acceptance with their parents or carers. Consider the nature of the account. Is he or she able to provide a clear, coherent and considered description of his or her own experiences? Does it appear that he or she would benefit from an opportunity to reflect upon his or her attachment history?

2. Use the quality of attachment measure (devised by Lucy Berliner and David Fine). It can be used to help assess the attachment pattern.

Ask the parent/carer:

1. What do you think the relationship between you and the child is like? Is it as you would like it to be, or are there aspects that worry you? (If it may be of help, describe the different patterns of attachment to the parent.)

2. What is your routine of care? (For example, mealtimes, bath times etc.)

3. What happens when you and the child separate? Does he or she show signs of over-anxiety, clinginess or indifference?

4. What do you usually do to comfort the child when he or she is distressed? Does this usually work?

5. Do you find that you can make time for your child?

6. (If the child is living away from home) do you feel that you have enough contact with your child? What do you understand the reason for the contact to be?

What are the wider resources that contribute to the child's attachment network?

Ask the parent/carer:

1. Could you name all the people (adult or child) that the child knows, or has known in the past, who you think are important to him or her?

2. Do you feel that you have enough support to be able to be a good parent? Is there anything that you think makes it difficult to parent, for example, lack of money, poor housing, lack of friends, lack of educational opportunities and so on?

3. Can you think of anybody that you know who may be able to spend some time with your child?

4. If the child does not attend any clubs or activities, do you think this would be of benefit?

QUALITY OF ATTACHMENT

This tool has been developed by Lucy Berliner and David Fine, Center for Sexual Assault and Traumatic Stress, Harborview Medical Center, Seattle, Washington and is reproduced with their permission. The process of detailed evaluation and validation of this material is currently underway. Modified versions may therefore be produced in the future.

Four short descriptions are provided which relate to each of the four types of attachment:

- secure attachment (Type B)

- insecure – avoidant (Type A)

- insecure – ambivalent (Type C)

- insecure – disorganised (Type D)

Simply ask the parent or carer to say which description best fits the child's attachment behaviour.

Child/adolescent smiles, and often seeks physical contact when greeting you; having you present relaxes child; s/he is usually comfortable when alone or separated from you. (B)

Child/adolescent appears independent, almost too independent for their age; s/he may avoid you; s/he is not upset at separation; child/adolescent is as comfortable with strangers as family members. (A)

Child/adolescent is clingy and anxious with you; gets upset when separated from you and may have difficulty being alone; s/he is glad to see you, but at the same time may act angry or upset. (C)

Child/adolescent may show a mixture of being distant and anxious; s/he can be angry and controlling or be compliant, but in an overly sweet/fake way. (D)

4

Education

Background information

Good educational attainment is associated with good outcomes and is therefore a protective factor that should be aimed for (Rutter 1991). School also offers a wide range of other opportunities to boost resilience, including acting as a complementary secure base, providing many opportunities for developing self-esteem and efficacy and opportunities for constructive contact with peers and supportive adults (Garbarino *et al.* 1992; Gilligan 1998).

It is now recognised that being accommodated away from home is likely to have a significant negative impact upon educational achievement (Jackson 1995; Parker *et al.* 1991). Government policy initiatives are aimed at this problem (Scottish Office 1999). There may be a temptation for practitioners to wait until the child is settled before attending to school issues. However, when a child is unsettled school could in fact be the main priority for intervention.

During school years children's cognitive development should be rapid. They become less egocentric (see also Positive Values domain). They move into what Piaget described as the concrete operational stage and should become better able to use logic and to make deductions about how the world works (Piaget 1952). During school years reading, in particular, is an essential skill to learn. Literacy is known to be valued especially highly by children who have experienced adversity and who have been accommodated by the local authority (Jackson 1995). Many young people who have 'succeeded from care' had discovered the pleasures of reading. This helps a child not only to learn, but also literally to enjoy him or herself, and can be a comforting activity throughout the life span.

The 'learning journey' for each child will be unique and strategies for intervention should incorporate realistic goals arising from a sound assessment, gradually building on small achievements for the child. There can be mutual stereotyping between social work and education. A climate of shared responsibility is needed in which information flows both ways. Expectations in school need to be reasonable, but not too high. Sometimes expectations are high of behaviour, but low of academic achievement. There is often a subculture among pupils within schools of not working and messing about (Meadows 1986). Children may need strategies to help them not get into trouble with others.

In order to establish what for each individual child will represent 'high but reasonable expectations' (also associated with achievement in disadvantaged children) the adult needs to be closely attuned to the child's capabilities and capacities. This requires careful observation and informs the more precise learning steps in the child's cognitive progress. Vygotsky's (1962) concept of 'scaffolding' would suggest that academic expectations need to be pitched just ahead of current achievement by someone with detailed knowledge of the child's ability. High achieving when leaving care is associated with having had the opportunity to develop a relationship with someone who believes in them and supports them. This often includes a healthy challenge in the face of poor effort.

Successful educational experiences are fostered by good home–school alliances. Some of the most basic skills that will help a child in the school setting can be learned at home. Some children will need extra help in learning because of early gaps or interruptions in their learning or overall development. Creative adults can find ways of linking the child's natural enthusiasm for an activity with habits of more formal learning, for example, harnessing a child's enthusiasm for football or another sport and incorporating basic scoring (maths) and practising and memorising the details of matches (memorising techniques). Harnessing the child's natural curiosity and enthusiasm is also a vehicle for encouraging play and social development in the older child.

Some parents will themselves have had difficult experiences of school. For them school may seem an intimidating place which triggers uncomfortable memories and it will be difficult for them to communicate effectively with the school without support. Parents who themselves have literacy problems may value the opportunity to learn in parallel with their children.

When assessing who has the potential to offer educational support, parents and other family members can be considered, even if children do not live with them. The most important issue is the need for someone to have detailed day-to-day knowledge of, and interest in, the child's development. Such a person could be a volunteer, mentor from the community, family member, keyworker in a residential unit, or the like.

It can be helpful to consider three different aspects of education:

- the school as a place
- education as a process
- educators as people.

Each of these aspects is important and it may be helpful to look at whether there are strengths or problems in each. For example, as a place school can, for some, be a haven of regularity and safety while for others it may be the site of bullying. For children with poor social skills (see Social Competencies domain), interaction with other children may be a source of stress and anxiety and may interfere with learning. For others it may be a source of friendship. For some children the process of learning is fun and challenging, for others it can seem threatening and frightening. Finally, the school staff, and particularly guidance teachers, form a pool of concerned adults among whom the child can find someone who is a source of emotional and/or intellectual support.

EDUCATION CHECKLIST
CHILD

First, it is necessary to have an up-to-date educational assessment and to identify any particular areas where extra support is needed. This assessment must be carried out by education staff and, where appropriate, an educational psychologist. Close cooperation with education staff is essential both during assessment and when planning and carrying out an intervention package. If the child is not attending school some of the questions will need to refer to previous experiences of school.

To what extent does the child show an interest in school and learning?

Ask the child:

1. Why do you think children have to go to school?

2. What do you think of your school? (If he or she has been to different schools ask how they compare, what did he or she like about each.)

3. If you could change something in your school, what would it be?

4. How do you feel when you go into the school building?

5. Do you find that you can concentrate in class? If not, why not?

6. What is your favourite subject or what do you enjoy learning about?

7. Who would you go to if you did not understand something in your favourite subject?

8. Who would you ask for help in your least favourite subject?

9. What would you most like to learn about next?

10. Do you think there is anything that you need extra help with, for example, reading?

11. What would you most like to achieve this term?

12. How do you get on with the other children at school?

To what extent does the parent or carer environment facilitate the child's learning and school attendance?

Ask the child:

1. Who knows what you are doing at school?

2. Who do you think takes an interest in your school progress?

3. How much do your parents and/or carers know about your school progress?

4. Do you have a private place to do your homework?

5. Who helps you with your homework?

6. Who goes to school meetings and who would you like to go school meetings?

What opportunities are there in the wider environment to support this child's education?

Ask the child:

1. Do you meet up with any of the children you know at school out of school? If not, would you like to be able to meet up with anyone more?

2. Is there any teacher in particular (or member of support staff) who you find easy to talk to and who helps you with school issues?

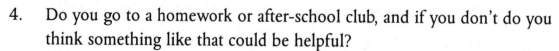

3. Is there anyone else that you know outside school who can help you with your schoolwork (for example an aunt or uncle, grandparent or friend)?

4. Do you go to a homework or after-school club, and if you don't do you think something like that could be helpful?

EDUCATION CHECKLIST
PARENT/CARER

To what extent does the child show an interest in school and learning?

Ask the parent/carer:

1. Do you have an accurate assessment of the child's current level of achievement? If not, who can help you with this from the school setting? Are you kept informed about your child's performance?

2. Do you think he or she understands the purpose of school?

3. How would you describe his or her experience of school, for example, positive, extremely variable, reluctant, avoidant, completely resistant?

4. What is the child's attitude to learning?

5. Do you think that he or she has a sense of belonging in school now or has had in the past?

6. Do you think that he or she is able to concentrate on school work?

7. What are the *child's* interests? Have these interests been linked with the child's time at school? If not, how might this be done?

8. What is this child good at?

9. If this child is described as slow or interrupted or delayed, what does this mean to you from your knowledge of the child? Do you think there is anything that he or she needs extra help with, for example, reading?

10. What would you most like your child to achieve this term?

11. How do you think that he or she gets on with the other children at school?

To what extent does the parent or carer environment facilitate the child's learning and school attendance?

Ask the parent/carer:

1. Who knows what the child is doing at school? Who tracks whether work is completed and to a satisfactory standard? Who supports his or her subject choices? Who helps with revision?

2. Who can/is helping you to set out activities, help and ideas focused on what he or she needs to learn next?

3. Who helps you with strategies for helping the child to learn? How are these strategies reviewed?

4. Does he or she have a private place to do his or her homework?

5. Who helps with homework?

6. Who attends school meetings? If you don't, would you like to be able to?

7. When was this child's last success at school? How was this marked or celebrated and by whom, at home and/or at school?

8. What were your own experiences of school?

9. Would you like access to educational opportunities yourself?

What opportunities are there in the wider environment to support this child's education?

Ask the parent/carer:

1. Does he or she meet up with any children from school out of school? If not, are there ways that this could be encouraged and supported?

2. Is there any teacher in particular (or member of support staff) that the child appears to have a good relationship with?

3. Is there anyone in the community who could act as a mentor in relation to his or her learning? Who could help them now by offering time and high, but reasonable, expectations of achievement?

4. Does he or she attend a homework or after-school club, and if not do you think something like that could be helpful?

5

Friendships

Background information

> From a remarkably early age, children not only can describe their various network associates, but can offer candid appraisals of the extent of support they expect from each. (Thompson 1995, p.34)

Resilience is associated with having generally positive peer relationships, and, specifically, good friendships (Werner 1990). Much research has been carried out about the importance of social support for adults and more is emerging about the importance of such social support for children. It is known that having friends can help buffer the effects of stress, prevent stress, mediate stress and provide information to deal with stress. The key issue for adults appears to be the perception of having support (Thompson 1995). The issues for children are similar, but there are unique features of their friendships due to developmental stage, autonomy and power. Friendships in childhood allow for horizontal (equal) relationships, which complement the vertical relationships they have with adults. This allows them to learn the social skills of interacting with equals, such as competition and cooperation and in this way children socialise each other (Schaffer 1996). Friends are also for fun and companionship: children enjoy activities much more if they are carried out with friends rather than non-friends (Foot, Morgan and Shute 1990, cited in Schaffer 1996). Hartup (1992) describes friendships as also providing:

- contexts in which to acquire or elaborate social skills

- self-knowledge and knowledge about others

- emotional support in times of stress

- the basis for future intimate relationships.

Conversely, the lack of friends during childhood is associated with a range of problems (Schaffer 1996):

- emotional problems

- immature perspective-taking ability

- less altruism

- poor social skills in group entry, cooperative play and conflict management

- less sociability

- poor school adjustment

- poorer school attainment.

There is likely to be a circular pattern whereby children who already show problems such as aggressiveness and poor social skills have difficulty in making friends and are therefore less likely to have the opportunity to learn better skills.

From a young age children need relationships with adults and with other children, so that they can develop a network of attachments (Holmes 1993). Although good peer relationships can compensate to some extent for poor attachment experiences, there is evidence of an association between the quality of attachments and the quality of friendships. Children with secure attachments tend to relate to peers in a positive and responsive way, whereas children with insecure avoidant attachments may show either aggression towards or detachment from peers (Howe 1995). Social support can buffer the effects of adversity, but maltreatment can impair peer relationships so that those who need social support the most are the least likely to have it (Thompson 1995). Therefore, children with insecure attachments to parents or carers, or who have been abused or neglected, may need extra help with peer relationships.

In early school years friendship is normally based on proximity and the peer network is highly dependent upon parents and carers. School greatly widens children's networks and as children get older they make more active efforts to develop a network that is built upon common interests (Smith and Cowie 1991). Children become more able to gauge their peers' emotional states and intentions and to tailor their own actions in response, thus giving scope for complex, cooperative play (Schaffer 1996). In school years girls' friendships tend to be one-to-one, close and intimate, while boys tend to play competitive and team games in larger groups. By 6½ children are 11 times more likely to play with a same-sex peer than an opposite sex peer and will avoid playing with those of the opposite sex (Golombok and Fivush 1994; Maccoby and Jacklin 1987).

Having other children to play with is not necessarily the same as having friends and children's concepts of friendships develop during school years. At about 9 or 10 children begin to be more choosy about their playmates. They become friends with others with whom they have shared values and things in common. From 11 onwards friendships become increasingly based on understanding, self-disclosure and shared interests (Smith and Cowie 1991). Children increasingly describe their friends in terms of their internal characteristics and when asked what a best friend is, children up to about 8 have been found to mention sharing common activities, living nearby and getting help. From 9 they will talk about admiring and being accepted by a friend and having shared values. As they enter early adolescence young people talk about loyalty, commitment, genuineness and intimacy (Bigelow and La Gaipa 1980). In early school years they are likely to name about four best friends, and this may increase to about seven during middle school years.

Children are quick to assess their peers' potential as friends. Children's own views of their peers show a marked consistency around five categories which have been described as popular, controversial, rejected, neglected or average (Coie and Dodge 1983):

1. Popular children lead in a cooperative way. They have better skills for joining group activities and do so in a friendly way that avoids conflict and is open to compromise. They show little aggression, are willing to share, can sustain interaction and have positive, happy dispositions.

2. Controversial children may have some leadership skills, but also fight and are disruptive to group activities. These children may therefore be admired, but feared at the same time.

3. Rejected children are disruptive, lack cooperative skills or leadership skills and are argumentative and antisocial. They make frequent attempts to join group activities but do so in an inappropriate, aggressive or pushy way. They lack social skills for interacting with peers, spend less time in cooperative play, and are often engaged in solitary activity or with younger or other unpopular children.

4. Neglected children are not aggressive, and they also lack cooperative or leadership skills. They tend to stay at the margins of group activity, waiting and watching.

5. Average children show reasonable social skills and take part in cooperative activities and group play.

Whereas neglected children may become accepted if moved to a different peer group, rejected children frequently remain rejected. A spiral pattern can occur whereby a child displays poor social skills, which leads to him or her being rejected. The rejection reinforces those antisocial characteristics such as aggression and the child is rejected again. Children who are rejected by their peers in childhood are more likely to develop psychiatric disorders at the time, to have school problems and to have a range of psychiatric and psychosocial problems in adulthood (Schaffer 1996). Rutter and Rutter (1993) suggest a number of reasons for these poor outcomes that illustrate the way that peer problems and other problems can interact and exacerbate each other:

1. Rejection in itself is stressful.

2. Lack of friends means a lack of social support, which has been shown to be a major buffer from psychiatric problems.

3. Lack of friends can cause a lack of involvement in school activities and other opportunities for personal development.

4. Peer rejection can lead to low self-esteem and poor self-efficacy.

5. The behaviour that is associated with peer rejection, especially aggression, may in itself be associated with later problems.

Being able to make friends is only part of the equation; the type of friendships made is another. Less association with delinquent peers and positive peer relationships have been found to be protective, an issue which becomes very important in adolescence (Fergusson and Lynskey 1996; Quinton *et al.* 1993).

FRIENDSHIPS CHECKLIST
CHILD

Remember that children of this age tend to play more with children of the same gender and that the play of the two genders is often different. However, it is also important not to make assumptions, especially as the more resilient children tend to conform less rigidly to traditional sex-roles. It may be that within school the child has mainly same-sex friends, but has a friend of the other gender out of school.

What characteristics does this child have that help with making and keeping friends?

1. Either give the checklist 'My friends and me as a friend' that follows to the child to fill in, or go through it with him or her. If this does not seem appropriate, or does not provide enough information, you could try the following.

2. Have a general chat with the child about how he or she gets on with other children, for example, simple scenarios can be used to see how the child enters a group. First find out what games the children in the school tend to play and which ones he or she enjoys, then say 'One day, when playtime starts you can't get out straight away and by the time you get to the playground some of your classmates have started to play (his or her favourite game). What would you do?'

3. To find out who the child's friends are, and whether he or she has any special friends you can simply ask the child.

4. You can also produce an ecomap: draw a circle in the centre of the paper to represent him or her and then add circles to represent children they know at the distances they indicate.

5. If you can get hold of a school class photo you can use it as a prompt as to who the child's friends are. Alternatively, if the school has individual

photos of children in the class you can ask the child to sort the photos into three piles of children 'I really get on with', 'I don't get on with at all', 'I get on with just OK'.

6. Ask the child to tell you what he or she thinks a friend is. If they cannot come up with an answer give some choices, such as 'someone you play with', 'someone who lives nearby', 'someone to have fun with', 'someone who likes the same things as you do', 'someone to help you if you have problems' and so on.

To what extent does the parent or carer environment facilitate the development of friendship?

Ask the child:

1. Do any of your friends ever come to your house to play?

2. Have you got any friends that are not through school, but are the children of your parent's friends or are cousins?

3. If you want to meet up with a friend, would your parent or carer help you, for example by making the arrangements, taking you to his or her house, and so on?

4. Is your parent or carer ever there when you are playing with friends, and if they are, what do they do if an argument breaks out?

What are the child's friendships like at the moment?

1. If at all possible arrange to observe this child playing with other children and see what proportions of time are spent in solitary, parallel and group play.

2. Does the child appear to have any particular friends?

3. Have a detailed discussion with the child's school teacher about the child's peer relationships. Describe the categories of popular, rejected, controversial, neglected and average and ask how the teacher thinks the other children in the class would categorise the child.

4. Ask the child: 'What opportunities are there for you to have contact with children other than at school, for example, are there local youth clubs or groups you can join or have joined?'

MY FRIENDS AND ME AS A FRIEND

You can write whatever you like in answer to each question. If you are not sure of what to put, just write that you aren't sure.

1. If you hear the word 'friend', what does it mean to you?

2. Why do you think people like to have friends?

3. What things about you would make people want to be your friend?

4. How many friends do you have?

5. How many of your friends are *best* friends?

6. What do you like about your friends?

7. Do you see your friends as much as you would like to?

8. Do you ever worry that you don't get on very well with other children?

9. What sort of things do you like to do with your friends?

✓

10. Are there any friends that you have not seen for ages, but would like to?

11. Do you ever find that other children won't let you join in their games?

12. Have any of your friends ever got you into trouble?

13. Do you have a friend that you can talk to about things that worry you?

14. Are you happy with the way things are with your friends, or is there anything that you would like to be different?

15. Who would you talk to about any problems that you have with any of your friends?

FRIENDSHIPS CHECKLIST
PARENT/CARER

What characteristics does this child have that help with making and keeping friends?

Ask the parent/carer:

1. How does this child get on with other children? Does he or she seem a lot shyer than other children, or a lot more pushy, or does he or she play well with others?

2. If we ask your child 'Who are your best friends?' what do you think he or she will say?

3. If we ask your child 'What is a friend?' what do you think he or she will say?

To what extent does the parent or carer environment facilitate the development of friendship?

Ask the parent/carer:

1. Do any of your child's friends ever come to the house to play?

2. Have any of your child's friends been made through you, for example with children of your friends or family?

3. How much would you get involved in any arrangements your child might make to see friends?

4. Do you get much chance to see how your child plays with other children? If so, how do you normally help your child to play nicely with other children?

5. Are you ever worried that your child seems too clingy, or is not interested in other children?

What are the child's friendships like at the moment?

1. Take some time to describe solitary, parallel and group play to the parent and then ask: 'Tell me about the way your child plays with other children, how much time do you think he or she spends in each of these different kinds of play?'

2. Say to the parent/carer: 'Sometimes children describe another children as a friend or best friend, but in fact the other child probably wouldn't see him or her as a friend. Would this be the case for your child, or does he or she seem to have at least one good friend?'

3. Describe the categories of popular, rejected, controversial, neglected and average and ask how they think the other children would categorise their child.

4. Ask what opportunities there are for the child to have contact with children other than at school, for example, are there local youth clubs or groups he or she can join or has joined?

6

Talents and Interests

Background information

Self-esteem is one of the fundamental building blocks of resilience. Self-esteem has been defined as: 'Appreciating my own worth and importance and having the character to be accountable for myself and to act responsibly toward others' (California State Department of Education, cited in Brooks 1994, p.547).

This definition highlights the importance of the interpersonal element of self-esteem. Having a healthy sense of self-esteem is not just about feeling good about oneself while having no regard for the impact of oneself upon others. Therefore, the goal of much long-term work with children is not only to help them to feel better about themselves, but also to help them recognise the importance of interrelationships and of empathy with others. Self-esteem appears to be linked with levels of self-efficacy which is also known to be associated with resilience and which is discussed in more detail in the Social Competence domain (Luthar 1991). So, children with high self-esteem have a realistic notion of their abilities and see successes as due to their own efforts and within their control. Those with low esteem are more likely to attribute any successes to chance. They see failures as due to un-changeable factors, for example a lack of ability or intelligence. They demonstrate a sense of helplessness and hopelessness, expect to fail and show self-defeating behaviour (Brooks 1994).

Harter (1985) suggests that self-esteem is based in the balance between what children would like to be and what they think they actually are. Everyone has an 'ideal' self and a 'perceived' self, and the closer they are to each other, the healthier the self-esteem (Schaffer and Emerson 1964). Self-esteem is not simply related to being good at something. A child may be very good at mathematics, but not value that skill. Also, a child who would like to be good at art, but perceives that his or her drawings are poor, will have a lower esteem than a child who does not value art and whose drawings are poor.

In her studies of self-esteem, Harter (1985) looked at a global measure of self-esteem (general self-worth) as well as five separate domains:

- scholastic competence
- athletic competence
- social acceptance
- physical appearance
- behavioural conduct.

Harter found the different domains to be independent of each other, so for example, a child might have a high score in one area and a low one in another. It is not until children reach the age of about 6 or 7 that a reliable, separate global rating of self-esteem can be measured (Harter 1985). Self-esteem can change and is amenable to improvement. During the school years the potential for boosting self-esteem, especially through activities at school, is great.

The roots of esteem lie firmly in early attachment experiences and enduring feelings based on early experiences of being loved. During the early years sensitive, warm and accepting parenting in the context of at least one secure attachment is fundamental to the development of good self-esteem. Studies of 10–11-year-old boys have shown high self-esteem to be associated with parents who have high self-esteem themselves and who are very accepting of their children and allow them freedom, but within clearly defined and enforced limits. Low self-esteem is associated with rejection and either authoritarian or permissive parenting (Coopersmith 1997). In school years, self-esteem is also affected by relationships with classmates, friends and teachers (Harter 1985).

Therefore, encouraging the child's unique talents and interests can help to boost resilience. If a child has a natural talent it should be nurtured and, more importantly, the child should learn to value that talent. If a child has an interest, that interest should be supported, even if the child has no special talent in the area. Many children who have experienced adversity and who may be either at home or 'looked after' may have hidden attributes and potential that have not emerged under conditions of stress and confusion. For example, children who are preoccupied with surviving abuse, or living with domestic violence, may have learned to use their energies in adapting to complex or changing family circumstances, and hence will not have had the chance or energy to make use of available opportunities. Those children and young people who adapt to stress and trauma by becoming passive or those with particularly low self-esteem, may have little or no sense of their own particular aptitudes. The challenge for practitioners is therefore to find ways of creating opportunities for young people to experience feelings of success, perhaps by looking for 'islands of competence' (Brooks 1994).

Remarkably, some children still demonstrate unusual capacities and abilities, even in the most stressful circumstances and here the *continuity* of opportunity through any necessary changes or transitions will be of real importance. For example, the child who shows skill in physical coordination, who has enjoyed gymnastics and yet has to leave home or move to another placement, will benefit from continuing with the activity if at all possible.

TALENTS AND INTERESTS CHECKLIST
CHILD

What talents does this child have and does he or she have any particular interests?

Remember that what the child is interested in, what he or she values and what he or she is good at might all be different. The value he or she places on a skill might also be influenced by peer and social pressure, particularly if it is not one socially associated with their gender (for example, a boy interested in dance).

1. Use the list of activities and hobbies that follows 'What can I do and what would I like to do?' to help identify areas of interest, value and skill. It may also be helpful to use magazines and catalogues to trigger ideas.

2. A scale for self-esteem also follows that can be used with the older children in this age range to help determine how good they feel about themselves.

Ask the child:

1. What hobbies, activities and other things are you interested in?

2. Is there anything that any of your friends do that you wish you could try?

3. What things that you do at the moment do you enjoy?

4. Are there things that you think you are pretty good at?

5. Are there things that you wish you were good at?

6. Are there any activities that you would like to try?

7. Is there anything that you used to do or be good at that you would like to try again?

Does the parent or carer environment encourage the development and expression of talents and interests?

Ask the child:

1. Is anyone in your family interested in the same things as you?

2. Does anyone in your family have a hobby that you share or that you would like to share?

3. Do you feel that your parents or carers help you to keep up with your interests (e.g. give you fees, take you to meetings etc.)?

4. How interested do you think your parent or carer is in the things you do?

What opportunities are there in the wider environment for the nurturing of this child's talents and interests?

Ask the child:

1. Can you think of anyone you know who might help you do something you are interested in, for example, grandparent, older sibling, uncle or aunt, friend's parent and so on?

2. Do you know of local hobby clubs or groups near where you live that you do, or would like to, attend?

3. Are there any clubs or activities at your school that you do, or would like to, attend?

4. Is there anyone else that you think could help you with your hobbies, for example, keyworker, teacher, social worker?

WHAT CAN I DO AND WHAT WOULD I LIKE TO DO?

Activity	Am pretty good at	Would like to try
sports		
art		
drama		
music		
martial arts		
dance		
gymnastics		
computing		
crafts		
modelling		
creative writing		
photography		
swimming		
fishing		
chess		
keeping pets/animals		
horse-riding		
keep-fit		
Scouts, Brownies or Guides, Boys'/Girls' Brigade, Woodcraft		
cycling		
skating/skateboarding/scooting		
hill walking		
cookery		
collecting		
skiing		
sailing		

The School Years, © Brigid Daniel and Sally Wassell 2002 © Iain Campbell 2002

SELF-ESTEEM

The Rosenberg Self Esteem Scale is in the public domain and can be copied.

Please read each statement. Then circle the letter indicating how much you agree or disagree with the statement.

	Strongly agree	Agree	Disagree	Strongly disagree
1. I feel that I am a person of worth. I am as good as anybody else.	A	B	C	D
2. I feel that there are a lot of good things about me.	A	B	C	D
3. I feel that I fail a lot.	A	B	C	D
4. I can do things as well as most other people.	A	B	C	D
5. I do not have much to be proud of.	A	B	C	D
6. I wish I had more respect for myself.	A	B	C	D
7. I feel useless at times.	A	B	C	D
8. Sometimes I think I am no good at all.	A	B	C	D
9. I like myself.	A	B	C	D
10. I am happy with myself.	A	B	C	D

Scoring for Rosenberg Self Esteem Scale

For questions 3, 5, 6, 7 and 8 apply the following points:

A 1

B 2

C 3

D 4

For questions 1, 2, 4, 9 and 10 apply the following points:

A 4

B 3

C 2

D 1

Add up the total number of points and divide by the number of questions to give the final score. The higher the score the higher the level of self-esteem.

TALENTS AND INTERESTS CHECKLIST
PARENT/CARER

What talents does this child have and does he or she have any particular interests?

Explain to the parent or carer that what the child is interested in, what he or she values and what he or she is good at might all be different and that you want to find out about all areas.

Ask the parent/carer:

1.   What hobbies, activities and other things is your child interested in?

2.   Can you think of any activities that your child seems to enjoy?

3.   Does your child show signs of having a particular skill or talent, for example, in art, sport and so on? If so, does he or she value that skill?

4.   Do you know what activities and skills that your child thinks it is important to be good at?

5.   Do you think there are any other activities that your child might enjoy trying?

6.   Can you think of anything that your child used to show signs of being good at in the past that could be picked up on again?

7.   How good do you think he or she feels about him or herself?

Does the parent or carer environment encourage the development and expression of talents and interests?

Ask the parent/carer:

1.   Are there activities that you enjoy, do you have time to take part in them, and could they be shared with your child?

2.   Does anyone in your family have a hobby that your child does, or could share?

3.   Do you find that you are able to help your child take part in activities? If not, what gets in the way, for example, lack of time, money or energy?

What opportunities are there in the wider environment for the nurturing of this child's talents and interests?

Ask the parent/carer:

1.   Can you think of anyone you know who might help your child do something he or she is interested in, for example, grandparent, older sibling, uncle or aunt, friends and so on?

2.   Do you know of local hobby clubs or groups near where you live that your child does, or would like to attend? If not, would you like help finding out this information?

3.   Do you know of any clubs or activities at your child's school that he or she does, or would like to, attend? Would you like more information about this?

4.   Is there anyone else that you think could help your child with hobbies, for example, keyworker, teacher, social worker?

7

Positive Values

Background information

Holding positive values and having the capacity to act in a helpful, caring and responsible way towards others is associated with resilience (Benson 1997; Raudalen 1991; Werner and Smith 1992). Such 'prosocial' behaviour is displayed in actions towards others that are not based on the expectation of external rewards (Smith and Cowie 1991) and include:

- helping others
- comforting others in distress
- sharing with others.

It is during school years that children will normally develop increasingly sophisticated moral reasoning (Kohlberg 1969). Up until about 9 years of age, children will tend to base their moral reasoning upon obedience to those in authority, have a limited understanding of the importance of a person's intention and tend to judge by outcome. For example, younger school-age children are likely to suggest a greater punishment for someone who accidentally breaks ten cups than for someone who deliberately breaks one. They will be operating at what has been called a 'preconventional' stage of moral reasoning (Kohlberg 1969). After this stage children move towards a 'conventional' morality. They have a greater understanding of the importance of intention and are increasingly able to take another's perspective. They would suggest a greater punishment for the deliberate breaking of one cup. Their understanding of mutual expectations is greater and of the importance of living up to what significant others expect of them. They develop understanding of notions of trust, loyalty, respect and gratitude. (See Appendix for more information about stages of moral reasoning.)

School-age children should have a 'theory of mind', that is they should know that other people have feelings and that other people's feelings about certain things may not be the same as their own. They should also have a language for feelings, both their own and others. As well as being able to describe situations that will generate feelings of happiness, sadness, anger, fear and shyness, in other words, emotions that tend to be shown in facial expressions, they can also describe situations that require more understanding of contextual factors, such as those that elicit pride, jealousy, worry, guilt and gratitude (Harris *et al.* 1987; Terwogt and Stegge 1998). The development of such empathy is a crucial building block for prosocial behaviour. Children of this age group should show the three components of empathy (Feschbach 1984):

> identifying the other's emotional state (affect identification), understanding the situation in which the other person is involved from that person's point of view (perspective taking), and experiencing in oneself the emotions felt by the other person (emotional responsiveness). (Feschbach 1984, p.197)

Children who exhibit empathy are less likely to demonstrate aggressive behaviour towards others (Goldstein 1999). They will have begun to internalise the parental/carer 'voice' as the basis of a conscience, and increasingly be able to inhibit their own antisocial behaviour without adult supervision. So, they should demonstrate that they are:

(a) Thinking or reasoning (problem-solving, decision-making) in a rational way

(b) Showing an awareness of, and consideration for, the needs, interests, and feelings of others as well as oneself

(c) Behaving constructively (i.e., in ways that benefit both self and others). (Goldstein 1999, p.305)

If these elements are not evident then it may be necessary to draw from the *Early Years* workbook for suggestions for intervention.

A child may be able to articulate what is 'right' and 'wrong', but may still do what is 'wrong'. However, because there does tend to be an association between a child's level of moral reasoning and their moral behaviour (Eisenberg *et al.* 1991; Goldstein 1999) it is important that it be taken into account when assessing elements of positive values. If a child often gets into trouble it will be necessary to explore separately whether he or she understands the difference between right and wrong and whether they are able to inhibit antisocial actions (the domain of Social Competence is intertwined with this domain).

There are several aspects of care-giving that are known to encourage the development of prosocial behaviour. Warm and secure attachment to a caregiver provides the basis for the development of empathy and for the understanding that others have feelings that can be influenced. If the attachment figure models kind behaviour then this is highly influential because children imitate people they identify with. Children also respond to clear rules and expectations of behaviour towards others. Parents with children who show prosocial behaviour tend to (Schaffer 1996; Zahn-Waxler, Radke-Yarrow and King 1979):

- provide clear rules and principles for behaviour, reward kindness, show disapproval of unkindness and explain the effects of hurting others

- present moral messages in an emotional, rather than calm manner

- attribute prosocial qualities to the child by telling him or her frequently that they are kind and helpful

- model prosocial behaviour themselves

- provide empathic care-giving to the child.

The indicator for mapping this area is the child's behaviour towards others. This can be assessed by direct observation, discussions with parents, teachers, keyworkers and carers, and conversations with the child. It should be possible to check the child's ability to take the perspective of others by, for example, using stories or play figures to create situations where something good or bad happens and exploring what the child thinks the subjects may have felt. Moral reasoning can be assessed by using simple vignettes posing moral dilemmas.

If a child is already demonstrating positive actions towards others then this is very hopeful. It indicates a level of empathy, which in turn can be linked with self-esteem and an understanding that other people have feelings. Therefore, prosocial behaviour should be reinforced wherever possible and intervention to boost resilience can be built upon existing positive values, for example, by involving children in helping in a community project.

If a child is not demonstrating positive values, then this should be considered a priority area for targeted intervention to boost resilience. The younger such behaviour can be encouraged the better, especially as there appears to be continuity between how kind a child is when young and when older (Dunn and Kendrick 1982). The ecological model is highly important here because the social environment exerts such a strong influence over children's social behaviour. Situations need to be created that require young people to care for and be responsible towards others. Raundalen (1991), for example, suggests that children's empathic behaviour can be enhanced through encouraging interest in the environment and nature and by giving opportunities for caring for pets.

Foster parents, teachers and other professionals in a caring role need to be able to put over the emotional messages when giving challenging messages about antisocial, unkind or cruel behaviour towards others. Although the professional role often requires calmness, and acceptance, this has to be balanced with the 'human' elements of an adult–child relationship that foster empathy and positive values.

The starting point should be an assumption that everyone has the potential to behave prosocially and that no matter what traumas have been experienced, all young people can learn to control antisocial behaviour.

POSITIVE VALUES CHECKLIST
CHILD

What level of moral reasoning does this child show, what understanding of his or her own feelings and what ability to empathise with those of others?

1. Use the moral dilemma that is provided below. It includes examples of possible replies at different levels of moral reasoning. Other dilemmas could be created as appropriate for the specific child. Discuss the dilemma with the child. Remember, it is the *reasons* that children give for their responses that tell you most about their moral reasoning, not the actual answer.

2. Choose situations from this child's own experience in which he or she has been in trouble for behaving antisocially, for example, where the child has stolen from a peer, or been involved in bullying. Have a discussion that focuses specifically on exploring the child's level of moral reasoning, for example, when a child has been caught stealing at school some questions could be:

    (a) Why do you think the teacher punished you?

         (example of 'preconventional' response: 'because I got caught';

         example of 'conventional' response: 'because I did wrong')

    (b) If you were the teacher, what would you have done?

         (example of 'preconventional' response: 'made me give the things back'; example of 'conventional' response: 'asked me why I did it')

    (c) What do you think the other child should have done?

         (example of 'preconventional' response: 'steal something of mine';

         example of 'conventional' response: 'tell the teacher')

(d) Why do you think children get punished for stealing?

(example of 'preconventional' response: 'because they get caught'; example of 'conventional' response: 'because if there were no rules against stealing nobody would be able to trust anybody').

3. Use the pictures 'Emotional faces' that follow to check the child's understanding of different emotions of both him or herself and in others.

4. Use the pictures 'Emotional scenes' that follow to prompt discussion about situations that evoke different emotions. Does he or she have the language to discuss emotions?

5. Use the 'Index of empathy' checklist that follows to assess how well the child is able to appreciate the position of others.

Ask the child:

1. Do you ever have difficulty in knowing what other people are feeling?

2. What sort of thing would make someone:

(a) happy

(b) sad

(c) angry

(d) afraid

(e) shy

(f) proud

(g) jealous

(h) worried

(i) guilty

(j) grateful?

What level of helping behaviour does this child show?

Ask the child:

1. Are there any chores that you have to do:

(a) at home

(b) in placement

(c) at school?

The School Years, © Brigid Daniel and Sally Wassell 2002 © Iain Campbell 2002

2.   Do you think there are other chores that you could do?

3.   Do you ever offer to help your parent or carer without being asked?

4.   Do you ever find it difficult to let your parent or carer know how you are feeling?

5.   What does your parent or carer do when you are:

   (a)   upset

   (b)   frightened

   (c)   angry

   (d)   happy?

What level of comforting or sharing or more general prosocial behaviour does this child show?

Arrange to observe directly the child in school or with a group of peers and look for examples of prosocial behaviour. For example, how does the child react when another child is upset or hurt; does he or she share with others; does the child help other children who are struggling with a game or task?

   Ask the child:

1.   Think about all the things that you are interested in and like; are there ways you could help another child or young person who is interested in the same things?

2.   Can you think of some ways in which you do help:

   (a)   people that you know

   (b)   local organisations (e.g. children's hospital, pet rescue etc.)

   (c)   other people in the world (e.g. charities, Red Nose Day etc.)?

3.   Are there any of these that you would like to do, if you don't already?

4.   Do you already do, or would you like to try any of these:

   (a)   gardening

   (b)   planting trees

   (c)   caring for animals

   (d)   gathering litter?

MORAL DILEMMA

You are in the cloakroom at school and you see a classmate take something from the school bag of another child. What would you do and why?

Options can include:

- tell the teacher

- tell the victim

- tell the child who took the thing that you saw him or her

- not tell

- join in and take things.

Explore the reasoning by posing a number of questions and dilemmas such as:

1. Is it wrong to steal, if so why?

2. Would it be more wrong if the victim was a friend of yours?

3. What if the thief was a friend?

4. What if everybody knows that the teacher sometimes blames the wrong person for things?

5. What if you know that the thief was on his or her last warning and would be excluded if they were caught?

6. What if the victim is well known to be a thief him or herself?

7. What if the victim is very rich and has lots of things, but never shares anything?

8. What if the thief says he or she will hit you if you tell?

EMOTIONAL FACES

Emotional faces legends

Happy

Sad

Frightened

Angry

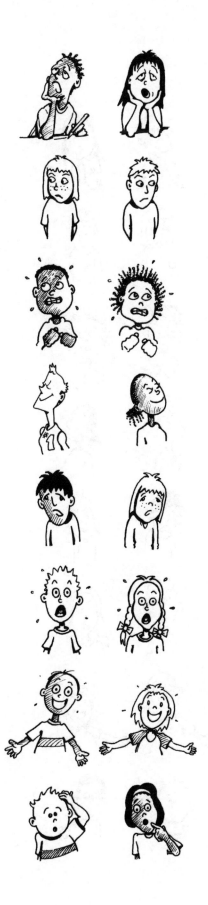

Emotional faces legends

Bored

Guilty

Anxious

Proud

Ashamed

Shocked

Surprised

Puzzled

The School Years, © Brigid Daniel and Sally Wassell 2002 © Iain Campbell 2002

EMOTIONAL SCENES

The School Years, © Brigid Daniel and Sally Wassell 2002 © Iain Campbell 2002

Emotional scenes legends

Frightened

Happy

Angry

Sad

AN INDEX OF EMPATHY FOR CHILDREN AND ADOLESCENTS

Adapted, with permission, from B. K. Bryant (1982) 'An index of empathy for children and adolescents.' *Child Development 53*, 413–425.

Administration

It is recommended that you go through the statements one-by-one with the child to make sure he or she understands them. Each reply should be marked as a YES or NO in the answer column. Take care with the statements that are framed negatively to be sure they are understood. Some statements are framed in the negative so that each one has to be thought about, and the child does not just answer YES to all. Do not try to add up the scores as you go along; do this afterwards.

Scoring

Using the scoring sheet, score 1 point for each YES reply to a positive (+) item and score 1 point for each NO reply to a negative (-) item. For the rest score 0. Then add all the scores up to give a final total out of 22.

As a guide, when this test was validated with children in the US (Bryant 1982) the average (rounded) scores were as follows:

Boys: Grade 1–12, Grade 4–11, Grade 7–13

Girls: Grade 1–14, Grade 4–14, Grade 7–16

Checklist

STATEMENT	RESPONSE YES or NO
1. It makes me sad to see a girl who can't find anyone to play with.	
2. People who kiss and hug in public are silly.	
3. Boys who cry because they are happy are silly.	
4. I really like to watch people open presents, even when I don't get a present myself.	
5. Seeing a boy who is crying makes me feel like crying.	
6. I get upset when I see a girl being hurt.	
7. Even when I don't know why someone is laughing, I laugh too.	
8. Sometimes I cry when I watch TV.	
9. Girls who cry because they are happy are silly.	
10. It's hard for me to see why someone else gets upset.	
11. I get upset when I see an animal being hurt.	
12. It makes me sad to see a boy who can't find anyone to play with.	
13. Some songs make me feel so sad I feel like crying.	
14. I get upset when I see a boy being hurt.	
15. Grown-ups sometimes cry even when they have nothing to be sad about.	
16. It's silly to treat dogs and cats as though they have feelings like people.	
17. I get angry when I see a classmate pretending to need help from the teacher all the time.	
18. Children who have no friends probably don't want any.	
19. Seeing a girl who is crying makes me feel like crying.	
20. I think it is funny that some people cry during a sad film or while reading a sad book.	
21. I am able to eat all my sweets even when I see someone looking at me wanting one.	
22. I don't feel upset when I see a classmate being punished by a teacher for not obeying school rule.	

Scoring sheet

STATEMENT	SCORE GUIDE	SCORE
1. It makes me sad to see a girl who can't find anyone to play with.	+ Score 1 for YES	
2. People who kiss and hug in public are silly.	- Score 1 for NO	
3. Boys who cry because they are happy are silly.	- Score 1 for NO	
4. I really like to watch people open presents, even when I don't get a present myself.	+ Score 1 for YES	
5. Seeing a boy who is crying makes me feel like crying.	+ Score 1 for YES	
6. I get upset when I see a girl being hurt.	+ Score 1 for YES	
7. Even when I don't know why someone is laughing, I laugh too.	+ Score 1 for YES	
8. Sometimes I cry when I watch TV.	+ Score 1 for YES	
9. Girls who cry because they are happy are silly.	- Score 1 for NO	
10. It's hard for me to see why someone else gets upset.	- Score 1 for NO	
11. I get upset when I see an animal being hurt.	+ Score 1 for YES	
12. It makes me sad to see a boy who can't find anyone to play with.	+ Score 1 for YES	
13. Some songs make me feel so sad I feel like crying.	+ Score 1 for YES	
14. I get upset when I see a boy being hurt.	+ Score 1 for YES	
15. Grown-ups sometimes cry even when they have nothing to be sad about.	- Score 1 for NO	
16. It's silly to treat dogs and cats as though they have feelings like people.	- Score 1 for NO	
17. I get angry when I see a classmate pretending to need help from the teacher all the time.	- Score 1 for NO	

18. Children who have no friends probably don't want any.	- Score 1 for NO	
19. Seeing a girl who is crying makes me feel like crying.	+ Score 1 for YES	
20. I think it is funny that some people cry during a sad film or while reading a sad book.	- Score 1 for NO	
21. I am able to eat all my sweets even when I see someone looking at me wanting one.	- Score 1 for NO	
22. I don't feel upset when I see a classmate being punished by a teacher for not obeying school rule.	- Score 1 for NO	
TOTAL SCORE		

✓

POSITIVE VALUES CHECKLIST
PARENT/CARER

What level of moral reasoning does this child show and what understanding of his or her own feelings and empathy with those of people close to the child?

Ask anyone who knows the child well about his or her understanding of morality. If necessary, describe the different stages of moral reasoning to them.

Ask the parent/carer:

1. To what extent do you think this child is able to understand why there are rules and sanctions or does he or she judge actions entirely by outcome?

2. Does this child show a respect for rules?

3. Does this child appear to understand the importance of the intention behind behaviour, in other words, can he or she distinguish between accidental and deliberate harm?

4. Does this child show an understanding of his or her own feelings, ability to talk about them and empathy with those of people close to them?

5. To what extent can this child take the perspective of others?

6. What emotions does this child appear to recognise in others?

7. What emotion words does this child have and are they used appropriately about him or herself?

What level of helping behaviour does this child show?

Ask the parent/carer:

1. Are there any chores that the child is expected to carry out:

   (a) at home

(b) in placement

(c) at school?

2. How does the child usually respond when asked to help?

3. Does the child ever spontaneously offer to help?

4. What do you do if the child does not help when asked?

5. Is this child able to let you know how he or she is feeling?

6. Does this child ever have difficulty knowing what others are feeling?

What level of comforting or sharing or more general prosocial behaviour does this child show?

Ask the parent/carer:

1. When this child is playing with other children how does your child react if another child is distressed, either because of his or her own or another child's actions or an accident? Have you seen your child try to comfort others?

2. Have you seen the child spontaneously share toys or activities with other children?

3. How does your child usually react if another child wants to share a toy or activity with him or her?

4. What opportunity can be created for this child to take responsibility for someone else's welfare, for example:

(a) mentor for newcomer at school

(b) helper for new child in residential unit

(c) guide for child new to activity in which this child is already skilled?

8

Social Competencies

Background information

The capacity for social competence has been demonstrated to be associated with resilience (Luthar 1991; Werner and Smith 1992). It is very difficult to pin down 'social competence' because it covers such a wide range of skills and attributes, many of them very closely intertwined with those associated with the Positive Values and Friendships domains. A useful definition is that developed by a Scottish Executive funded initiative, the Promoting Social Competence project based at Dundee University (Promoting Social Competence 1999):

> Social Competence is possessing and using the ability to integrate thinking, feeling and behaviour to achieve social tasks and outcomes valued in the host context and culture.

The definition goes on to incorporate:

> perception of relevant social cues, interpretation of social cues, realistic anticipation of obstacles to personally desired behaviour, anticipation of consequences of behaviour for self and others, generation of effective solutions to interpersonal problems, translation of social decisions into effective social behaviours, and the expression of a positive sense of self-efficacy.

Bernard (1991) identifies a group of factors that indicate resilience:

- social competence
- autonomy, also known as internal locus of control
- capacity for problem-solving
- sense of purpose and future.

The foundations for social competence are laid in early childhood. During early years children begin to develop autonomy and self-control. They learn about social and moral rules and compliance with parental expectations. They become better at directing their attention, focusing their attention and persisting in attendance on tasks (Masten, Best and Garmezy 1990).

During school years a child's sense of self-efficacy is crucial to social and academic success. The foundations of self-efficacy are laid down in early years, but during school years there are numerous opportunities for it to be moderated by experience. The development of self-efficacy depends in part upon the development of accurate explanations for events and the behaviour of oneself and others. These 'attributions', as they are known, have three components (Peterson and Seligman 1985). The first is whether the cause for an event is attributed to internal characteristics of the person, or to external, situational factors. For example, a child bumps into another child who could make the internal attribution 'They've deliberately hurt me', or the external attribution 'They've accidentally slipped'. The second component is whether the cause is seen as stable over time or transient: 'I'll avoid him because he's always going to have it in for me' or 'Usually I get on with him fine'. The third component concerns whether the cause is seen to apply globally or specifically: 'Other children are going to try and hurt me' or 'this was a one-off'. As they mature children need to develop reasonably accurate attributions about their own and others' behaviour. Children who have suffered abuse or severe loss often develop attributions that are internal, stable and global: 'It's my fault, it's going to last forever and it will affect everything I do'.

During school years, therefore, children need to develop a reasonably accurate assessment of their own and other people's ability. They also develop the ability to take account of the situation and how different people can be affected by different situations. Accurate social perception will help with social competence. They should be learning to control their instant impulses and to consider the best of a number of options in social situations.

During school years and as children enter adolescence socially appropriate conduct is expected:

> One of the most important criteria by which children are evaluated by adults in their society is by their conduct with respect to rules or social norms for behaviour, the expectations teachers have for conduct in the classroom and on the playground, and the laws of society governing conduct. Children are described as well-behaved rather than disobedient, antisocial, or delinquent according to their compliance with these norms for social behaviour. (Masten *et al.* 1990, p.120)

Lack of social competence can be shown in different ways. Some children are very withdrawn and lack the confidence and ability to engage with other children and find it very difficult to communicate effectively with adults. Such children are likely to have a low sense of self-efficacy and to lack communication and social skills. They may not attract the same level of attention as other children, but their need for intervention is great. For example, children who have been neglected may develop a pattern of withdrawal: in order to boost their resilience and to compensate for lack of social stimulation they are likely to benefit from help with social competencies (Crouch and Milner 1993).

Other children show high levels of aggression which mean that they fall out with their peers and are often in trouble with adults. During school years the levels of instrumental aggression (that is aggression aimed at getting what you want) normally declines. During school years children's aggression may also be associated with peer group activity. As older children develop the ability to put themselves in another's place and to understand the reasons behind other people's actions there should be a reduction of aggression. However, for children lacking in social competencies, aggression can become more subtle and deliberately planned (Schaffer 1996).

If a child is showing rule-breaking behaviour in school years, it is very likely to persist into adolescence, unless there is prompt and appropriate intervention (Masten *et al.* 1990). There is a strong association between academic achievement and rule-governed behaviour, but the direction of causality is not clear. Low IQ and lack of achievement could lead to frustration and alienation and therefore aggressive and antisocial behaviour. Alternatively, aggressive and antisocial behaviour could interfere with learning processes. It seems that for younger children the direction is that academic problems may be more likely to cause antisocial problems and therefore early intervention with learning problems is an essential part of prevention of social competence difficulties (Maston *et al.* 1990).

Social skills are usually learnt initially within the context of attachment relationships and are then extended to peers and other adults. In order to develop appropriate social skills children require an authoritative parental environment where warmth and sensitivity is coupled with the provision of clear boundaries and requirements for behaviour. Antisocial behaviour is associated with a parenting style that is harsh, punitive, rejecting and inconsistent (Coie and Dodge 1998).

Social skills involve cognitive, affective and behavioural aspects, therefore, when assessing them there needs to be attention to the *cognitive* areas like:

- planning and decision-making
- understanding cause and effect
- reflection
- problem-solving

affective areas like:

- empathy
- ability to take the perspective of others
- pleasure in having friends

behavioural areas like:

- interpersonal competence
- able to inhibit instinctive response
- conflict resolution.

SOCIAL COMPETENCIES CHECKLIST
CHILD

As described in the introduction, the term 'social competence' covers a wide range of cognitive, affective and behavioural factors. The focus here will primarily be upon cognitive and behavioural aspects of social competence because the affective aspects are essentially assessed in the Positive Values domain. Peer relationships are obviously a crucial indicator of social competence and although touched on here are assessed in detail in the Friendships domain.

To what extent do this child's personal characteristics contribute to his or her level of social competence?

Use the provided Social Attributes Checklist (McClellan and Katz 1992) to help with the assessment of this domain.

Ask the child about the following aspects of social competence.

AUTONOMY

Do you like to try to do things for yourself and make some of your own decisions (for example, deciding what to wear, making arrangements to see friends, getting up in the morning, deciding what to spend pocket money on)?

SELF-CONTROL/PROBLEM-SOLVING

1. Do you ever worry that you can't control your temper?

2. Do you ever find yourself hitting out at other children without really thinking about it?

3. Do you ever feel that you don't show your feelings enough?

4. Do you ever feel that you show your feelings too much?

5. When you are in a difficult situation, can you usually think of different ways you could react and decide which seems the best (for example, if you suspect that a classmate has stolen something of yours choices might be to confront him or her; tell the teacher; speak to a parent or carer; check with other friends what they think, and so on)?

TEMPERAMENT

1. Do you think of yourself as a cheerful sort of person?

2. What kind of sense of humour do you have (for example, do you make jokes, do you usually get other people's jokes)?

3. If something goes wrong for you, like you lose at a game, do you usually get over it quite quickly, or does it take you a long time to stop feeling upset?

4. If an adult you don't know very well, perhaps a teacher of another class or a distant relative, says hello to you, how do you usually feel (for example, shy, pleased, nervous, chatty)?

SELF-EFFICACY

The 'Internal/External Locus of Control Scale' can be used as a gauge for the level of self-efficacy that the child shows. Either use it in full as it stands, or use it as a basis for areas to discuss.

ATTENTION

1. Do you find that you get distracted easily from things like working at school, or watching the TV?

2. Are you usually able to concentrate on a difficult task until it is finished?

To what extent does the parent or carer environment encourage social competencies?

Ask the child:

1. What sort of rules are there in your house about getting on with each other (for example, saying 'please' and 'thank you', answering when spoken to or asked a

question, being told not to interrupt others, asking for things you want rather than grabbing them)?

2. How do your parents or carers usually react if you do something wrong? Do they explain to you why it is wrong, what sort of punishments do you get, do you usually know what things will annoy them?

What opportunities does this child have to develop competence in a wider social environment?

Ask the child:

1. Do you spend as much time as you would like with other children your age?

2. Do you usually get on OK with other children?

3. Do you find that you fall out with friends easily?

4. What do your parents or carers do or say if you fall out with your friends?

5. Can you usually get through the school day without being told off for something?

6. Do you find the school rules easy to keep (for example, if there is a uniform, not eating in class, not shouting out, lining up when told, and so on)?

SOCIAL ATTRIBUTES CHECKLIST

This checklist (McClellan and Katz 1992) is available on the internet from the ERIC Digest at http://www.ed.gov/databases/ERIC_Digests/index/. Items on the digest are for public use and there is a range of articles relating to resilience that may be of use.

Individual attributes

The child:

1. Is USUALLY in a positive mood

2. Is not EXCESSIVELY dependent on the teacher, assistant or other adults

3. USUALLY comes to the program or setting willingly

4. USUALLY copes with rebuffs and reverses adequately

5. Shows the capacity to empathise

6. Has positive relationship with one or two peers; shows capacity to really care about them, miss them if absent, etc.

7. Displays the capacity for humour

8. Does not seem to be acutely or chronically lonely.

Social skills attributes

The child USUALLY:

1. Approaches others positively

2. Expresses wishes and preferences clearly; gives reasons for actions and positions

3. Asserts own rights and needs appropriately

4. Is not easily intimidated by bullies

5. Expresses frustrations and anger effectively and without harming others or property

6. Gains access to ongoing groups at play and work

7. Enters ongoing discussion on the subject; makes relevant contributions to ongoing activities

8. Takes turns fairly easily

✓

9. Shows interest in others; exchanges information with and requests information from others appropriately

10. Negotiates and compromises with others appropriately

11. Does not draw inappropriate attention to self

12. Accepts and enjoys peers and adults of ethnic groups other than his or her own

13. Interacts non-verbally with other children with smiles, waves, nods, etc.

Peer relationship attributes

The child is:

1. USUALLY accepted versus neglected or rejected by other children

2. SOMETIMES invited by other children to join them in play, friendship and work.

The School Years, © Brigid Daniel and Sally Wassell 2002 © Iain Campbell 2002

INTERNAL/EXTERNAL LOCUS OF CONTROL SCALE

The Nowicki-Strickland Internal/External Locus of Control Scale has been adapted into a shorter form for children. Reproduced with the permission of Steve Nowicki.

I'd like to ask you some questions now. There are no right or wrong answers. I'm just interested in knowing what you think and feel about different things.

	YES/NO
Do you feel that wishing can make good things happen?	
Are people nice to you no matter what you do?	
Do you usually do badly in your school work even when you try hard?	
When a friend is angry with you is it hard to make that friend like you again?	
Are you surprised when your teacher praises you for your work? (Prompt: if children say teacher hasn't praised them yet, ask about previous teacher – and note down in comments below)	
When bad things happen to you is it usually someone else's fault?	
Is doing well in your class work just a matter of 'luck' for you?	
Are you often blamed for things that just aren't your fault?	
When you get into an argument or fight is it usually the other person's fault?	
Do you think that preparing for tests is a waste of time?	
When nice things happen to you is it usually because of 'luck'?	
Does planning ahead make good things happen?	
Comments	

Internal/External Locus Of Control Scale Scoring

First reverse the score of the last question, i.e. if the child says 'yes' to the last question, change it to 'no'. Then count up the number of 'yes' replies and the number of 'no' replies.

EXTERNAL Locus of Control (i.e. child tends to see events as being controlled by external forces, has a low sense of self-efficacy) is associated with having more 'YES' scores.

INTERNAL Locus of Control (i.e. child tends to see him or herself as having some control over events, has a high sense of self-efficacy) is associated with having more 'NO' scores.

SOCIAL COMPETENCIES CHECKLIST
PARENT/CARER

To what extent do this child's personal characteristics contribute to his or her level of social competence?

The Social Attributes Checklist can be used with the parent or carer to find out their view of their child's social competence.

Ask the parent/carer about the following aspects of social competence.

AUTONOMY

What opportunities are there for your child to try things for him or herself and to make some of their own decisions (for example, deciding what to wear, making arrangements to see friends, getting up in the morning, deciding what to spend pocket money on etc.)?

SELF-CONTROL/PROBLEM-SOLVING

Does your child exert some measure of control over his or her behaviour, at a level that can normally be expected of a school-age child, does he or she show excessive levels of aggression? Does he or she appear to have any level of control over different possible reactions to a given situation?

TEMPERAMENT

Is your child normally cheerful, does she or he demonstrate a sense of humour, can he or she be comforted after a set-back, does he or she respond openly to overtures from adults and so on?

SELF-EFFICACY

The parent or carer can be asked how they would consider the child would rate on each item of the 'Internal/External Locus of Control Scale'.

ATTENTION

Can your child concentrate for periods of time on a particular task, can the child be encouraged to read a book, will he or she watch a video right through, will he or she make a number of attempts to complete a difficult task?

To what extent does the parent or carer environment encourage social competencies?

Ask the parent/carer:

1. What aspects of social behaviour do you believe to be important and how do you encourage such behaviour (for example saying 'please' and 'thank you', responding when greeted or asked a question, learning not to interrupt others, looking at people when they address him or her, turn-taking in conversation and games, asking for things he or she wants rather than grabbing them)?

2. What is your approach to discipline (for example, do you explain the reasons for your decisions, can you separate disapproval of the behaviour from feelings about the child)?

What opportunities does this child have to develop competence in a wider social environment?

Ask the parent/carer:

1. Does this child have the opportunity to play with other children of about his or her own age?

2. How would you deal with a situation where the child has fallen out with a friend?

3. How well does the child respond to other adults, is he or she very shy, or overly friendly?

4. Does the child appear to understand the school rules and conventions?

5. Does the child manage to keep to the school rules and conventions in a reasonable way?

Part II

Intervention

9

Intervention Strategies

Introduction

It is beyond the scope of these workbooks to give comprehensive intervention guidance. By its very nature, practice that aims to promote resilience has to be individually tailored to suit each individual child or young person and his or her unique circumstances. Instead, principles to underpin the planning of intervention are outlined and for each domain examples of possible intervention strategies are provided. Practitioners are encouraged to be as creative as possible in developing these strategies further to meet individual needs.

The balancing act

It can be difficult to decide whether to build upon existing strengths or whether to concentrate on boosting areas of less strength. Five strategies for intervention have been suggested (Masten 1994):

- reduce vulnerability and risk
- reduce the number of stressors and pile-up
- increase the available resources
- mobilise protective processes
- foster resilience strings (where an improvement in one domain has a positive knock-on effect in other domains).

We would recommend that practitioners strive to strike a balance between these different approaches. Current practice is frequently characterised by risk reduction and therefore more attention may need to be paid to looking for strengths and building upon them. Wherever possible a strength in one domain can be used to boost a weaker domain. For example, if a child has a strong attachment to a member of the extended family (Secure Base = strong), but takes part in no activities or hobbies (Talents and Interests = weak), the attachment figure can be encouraged and supported in helping the child to take part in an activity. Similarly, if a child has a good friend (Friendships = strong), but misses a lot of school (Education = weak), consideration could be given to involving the friend in encouragement to attend, perhaps by arranging for them to travel together.

The holistic approach

The resilient child can be described as one who can say (Grotberg 1997):

I HAVE

I AM

I CAN

For example, the child can say 'I have people who love me and people to help me', 'I am a likeable person and respectful of myself and others' and 'I can find ways to solve problems and can control myself'. The three categories loosely equate with the three building blocks of secure base, self-esteem and self-efficacy. The aim of intervention would be to develop all the domains so that the child can make such positive statements about him or herself:

I HAVE: this could be boosted via work on Secure Base and Friendships

I AM: this could be boosted via Positive Values and Social Competencies

I CAN: this could be boosted via Education and Talents and Interests.

The ecological approach

As has been stressed throughout the workbook, consider interventions at each ecological level. The following practice suggestions are grouped, as far as possible, into each ecological level, although there may well be considerable overlap.

Multi-agency, network approach

Finally, it is essential that the social worker does not attempt to carry out work on all the domains alone.

Any professional involved with the child and family must be involved in any planning discussions about boosting resilience and there must agreement about priorities and how to address them. For example, a residential keyworker may take the main role in working on talents and interests, but the school should also be informed of what these talents and interests are so that they can reinforce them.

The whole of the child's network of family and friends should be assessed for potential to help with boosting resilience. For example, a grandparent may be able to offer time to help with homework, or a friend's parent may be able to include the child on outings if given some financial help.

PRACTICE SUGGESTIONS
SECURE BASE

This domain of resilience acts as a focus for deliberate strategies fundamental to basic care routines for the child. These often simple strategies, applied with persistence and consistency, can strengthen the child's feeling of basic security and belonging. They may be introduced as a way of improving existing attachment relationships, or to help with the development of new ones. Although it is important for the child to be attached to the main carer, this should not preclude attention to relationships with other important people in the child's life. The improvement of attachment relationships will be most likely to promote healthy developmental progress and recovery from the impact of adversities. We need to examine:

- the existing sense of a secure base within the child, and

- existing strengths in the family setting which can be harnessed, but also

- existing strengths in the community and professional resources.

A useful paradigm, as described above, defines the resilient child as one who can make positive statements on each of three areas (Grotberg 1997):

I HAVE

I AM

I CAN

These three perspectives link particularly directly with interventions around the provision of a secure base, that is, when building security and predictability for children. Promoting a sense in children that they have relationships with significant people available to them and have a supportive environment, is clearly relevant in the deliberate structuring of elements of the child's environment focused on increasing a sense of security. Such interventions mirror the functions of a secure or 'good enough' attachment relationship that acts to reduce anxiety and to promote healthy exploration and learning in the child at every stage of their development. They are highly relevant for work with school-aged children who may have lost their secure base or who never experienced predictability and security of care at home. Many children at this stage of development are beginning to reflect on their circumstances, even if not in a verbally explicit fashion and their behaviour is often fuelled by this reflection. For example, 'I have been taken away and it is because I am naughty or too difficult for adults to handle'.

Every element of the child's environment may act to reassure the child that he or she has available to them a net of security such as to communicate messages:

'I have reliable predictable adults available to me to offer support.'

'I have a reliable routine.'

The second helpful concept is the focus on the promotion of a sense of healthy identity as expressed in the phrase 'I am'. Attachment to a person who values the child for his or her intrinsic qualities will facilitate the development of good self-esteem, that is the ability to say 'I am a person worthy of love and attention'.

Care-givers need to make detailed attempts to structure the child's immediate care environment so as to make it possible for him or her to *achieve* in even a small way some aim which has salience for them. This may have particular importance, for example, for a child who has no sense of initiative and such a poorly developed sense of self-concept that he or she does not even know what they enjoy and are capable of. We know that a sense of achievement is an important component of self-esteem, and that this is facilitated by the messages of acceptance communicated by all the elements of a secure base.

Finally, it is possible to progress from the notion of 'I have' in relation to basic security, to 'I can' in relation to achievement. In other words, the child who has a basic sense of security, is more likely to feel that he or she can attempt new tasks and explore the environment in the search for mastery, and later incorporate these positive experiences into a confident self-identity. This requires the integration of experiences, opportunities, successes and problem-solving skills to the point where the child perceives these capacities and abilities as part of him or herself, not merely as a function of chance or a particular setting. It also provides a chance to establish and reinforce for each child a sense of *mastery* and *autonomy*. This relates very closely to the notion of self-efficacy in that the child who is confident in his or her ability is more likely to feel 'I can do something about the problems and difficulties I face'.

Whether the child is at home or looked after by the local authority, a useful framework for planning intervention may be represented by the following questions:

1. What has happened to this child?

2. What have been the messages to the child in life events, relationships and circumstances?

3. What behaviour do we see, especially in persistent patterns?

4. What is this behaviour communicating?

5. What do we want to communicate?

6. How might we do this:

    (a) in the care routines for the child

    (b) in any direct work which is done with the child?

This provides a simple framework for reflection on the source of the behaviour problems. It is often helpful to separate intervention into addressing:

- the care routines or environment which need to be created for the child

- the ways that positive behaviour can be promoted to build resilience

- the explanations that need to given to the child and the best way to give them.

The aim is to move away from the emphasis on problems towards a focus on the child's positives and strengths.

Helping the child to feel secure

1. Shape interventions deliberately in response to the child's attachment style, and remember that persistence will be required. For example, a child who avoids contact (avoidant attachment pattern) will need patiently available carers who do not press the child to come

close but whose availability to offer support is nevertheless predictably present. A child who shows a combination of high levels of need for the carer combined with angry resistance (ambivalent attachment pattern) needs carers who have the patience and fortitude to withstand the demand and rejection: they need to help the child through the urge to reject closeness. A child whose responses are confused (disorganised attachment pattern) will need carers who can tolerate mixed responses and who are reliable and reassuring in their own responses. A child who shows clinging, anxious preoccupation with presence of the attachment figure (anxious attachment pattern) needs reassurance of carer responses that are as *predictable* as it is possible to provide, with only gradual encouragement in surviving brief separations.

2. School-aged children particularly enjoy sharing jokes with adults and this can promote a feeling of closeness and security in the known response of available adults (Dunn 1993). Some parents may benefit from opportunities to have shared fun with their children, for example on outings.

3. Any activity that promotes a sense of shared fun is important as some children will have experienced little pleasure in play or other activities and little sense of enjoying themselves. Any ordinary play experience can provide opportunities for this, for example, water play, modelling with clay, and so on.

4. As children's attachment relationships improve, so they should begin to show more discrimination between known and unknown adults. But if they do not, then all adults who come into contact with the child should be advised to model appropriate behaviour, for example, if a child is overly friendly with the social worker at first meeting the worker can say: 'I think we should check whether mum/dad/carer is happy for you to chat with me – you ask them'. When meeting new people the parent or carer can use phrases such as 'Now, you don't know XX very well yet, but if we chat a bit we can get to know them better' and so on. Care must be taken to protect such children from unscrupulous adults.

5. The parent or carer should take every opportunity, not only to *respond* to the child's demonstrated distress and to support him or her when under stress but also to *reach out* to the child to initiate positive experiences (Fahlberg 1991). It is not helpful simply to wait for the child to voice concerns, as many children will find this too difficult. It

is vital that the carer or parent takes initiatives to protect the child from undue negative effects of adverse circumstances.

6. When trying to understand any messages the child may be giving about his or her assumptions as to why he or she is not at home, why someone important has left, or the reasons for any other negative life events, help the parent or carer to reflect upon the child's *behaviour*, as well as what he or she *says*. Initiatives that encourage *reflection* with the child about the reasons for decisions or life events can be powerfully protective against later difficulties. During school years children may appear to have a greater understanding about events, but may still be prone to self-blame and false beliefs. Simple books about feelings using stories of children who have experienced difficulties, for example divorce, and have encountered strong feelings within themselves can be reassuring.

7. Many children explore through their play or drawings events that have troubled them or about which they feel great confusion. An opportunity for the child to lead the play can promote the communication of his or her worries and confusions and give the adult an opportunity to understand what the child has made of previous life events.

8. Any way in which the adult can communicate an *acceptance* to the child of his or her individuality is likely to be of great value. For example, simple activities like drawing around the child's body outline on paper and colouring in the child's particular features can provide an opportunity for positive acknowledgement of his or her attributes.

9. The importance of physical care is clear, not only in the provision of nourishing food, but also helping the child to care for him or herself in an age-appropriate way. During school years children should become more independent, but may appreciate still having things done for them sometimes.

10. Equally the provision of reliable medical attention for particular needs or conditions that may have been neglected gives positive messages to the child and offers chances for physical closeness. Non-abusive, nurturing touch can be deeply comforting to a child who has had physical or sexually abusive experiences.

Ensuring that the child has a secure base

1. Building healthier attachment relationships may be the most important initiative which, through work with parent and child separately or the parent and child relationship directly, can make a real difference to the child's sense of security.

2. An essential element of a secure base for children is predictability of care. Steady routines can have a deeply reassuring affect and the reliable availability of those important to the child provides a sense of belonging. Children need a balance between, on the one hand healthy limit setting and predictable routines of care and, on the other encouragement to take initiatives and explore the environment safely. Spend time with the parent or carer exploring the caring routines. For example, particular attention can be paid to providing enjoyable mealtimes as in some families these have been fraught occasions for the children. During school years the mornings may be particularly chaotic, especially if the child is reluctant to get ready for school. Looking at the morning routine in detail can show up the specific trigger points.

3. For many children who are insecure, for those who have separated from important adults, and particularly for children whose development is delayed, experiences geared at *exploring the senses* can be powerfully therapeutic. Sensory experiences are the way in which young children experience the world and play opportunities of this kind, for example, using dough, paints, water, music can be deeply reassuring. These can be helpful ways of relaxing very anxious children and beginning to teach them simple ways of calming themselves which will be an invaluable personal resource in later life.

4. Interest in the child's activities, encouragement of the child to take initiatives in play and development of the child's autonomy, will also build self-esteem.

5. The child who has difficulty separating needs to develop trust in the carer which can be encouraged by leaving the child for short periods with a known adult. Children of this age need explanations and reassurance about separation. As the child's trust grows, so longer separations can occur. The child should not be 'tricked' by the carer disappearing without any explanation.

6. Any play experience which can be constructed by a trusted adult to help a child to anticipate a difficult experience, and to play it out using objects of any kind, can help the child prepare him or herself for a stressful event. For example, for the child who is going to hospital it can help greatly to use the natural medium of play to predict some of the experiences the child is likely to have, and to offer reassurance. Encouragement to take an object from home and to be reassured of the availability of important adults will protect against the young child's sense of powerlessness and anxiety. It can also provide an opportunity for the expression of feelings that can be legitimised and supported by the adult.

7. Taking opportunities for special rituals for each individual child, at Christmas or other religious festivals, on their birthday and in celebration of significant achievements or events can build a trusting relationship between the child and any significant adult.

8. Any initiative and work with parents that helps them to learn about the developmental stage and actions they can take to increase the child's sense of security will be invaluable. For example, reliable, predictable routines are often underestimated by parents who themselves have had poor experiences of nurturing and group work support can help parents to understand about children's needs. It is likely that a combination of interventions that encourage direct positive engagement with the children in structured play sessions or nurturing tasks, with an opportunity for reflection with other parents is likely to be more successful than either initiative on its own. One approach to group work focuses on helping parents to change the kind of attributions they make about their children's behaviour.

9. Any initiative, however small, which communicates to the child that the adult has *space* and *time* for him or her and that they are unique and special in their own way, is likely to communicate a message of positive regard. Predictable periods of time spent with the child by a caring adult offering praise and encouragement and affirmation can be of vital significance, for example, by the regular telling of stories or engaging in special activities that have meaning for the individual child.

10. Whatever the child's living setting, he or she will need the comfort of contact with important people from his or her past and present: to have a notion that 'I have adults available to me when I need them'. Contact, if the child is separated from attachment figures, needs to be *purposeful*

so that it aims to meet the child's needs. It is also important to consult with the family about *how* contact can be prepared for and effectively managed. Many parents find it very difficult to be in a false setting for contact with their child, so careful consideration of venue, activities, and timing will be important in promoting the most effective contact for the child. Active gaining of *permission* from parents is vital here, even if it takes time, as it can consolidate the secure base both in the present placement and future care settings if the child knows that the parent is able to communicate their approval.

11. Take photographs of important shared experiences; these provide a sense of continuity for the child and reminders of important people and experiences. Photographs, tapes, drawings and videos can all help to keep important memories of life for children and remind them of their roots and sense of belonging in their community.

12. More work may need to be done with the adults, for example, when there are warring, separated parents, than directly with the children in establishing the child's right to contact with an important person who has left the household.

Capitalising upon the wider resources that are available as an attachment network

1. Enjoyable outings with a trusted adult can extend the child's world, giving them an opportunity to explore the environment and increasing the range of stimulation.

2. Base deliberate plans for care and contact upon careful attention to children's wishes and feelings to counteract both feelings of powerlessness and those of self-blame. Take care in thinking through with the child wherever possible *who* is important so that opportunities to sustain and build important attachments can be maintained, despite separations.

3. It may be that important people to the child are overlooked when making the care plan, or their significance minimised. It may be assumed that the child's mother is more important when a grandparent or father may be of real significance. Make no assumptions about who has something to offer the child.

4. Assess the nature and strength of sibling bonds and reassess this in the light of reparative work and care. For example, for a sibling group

where conflict has been a necessary adaptation to difficult family circumstances, or where there is an unhelpful allocation of roles to individual children, special attention to building mutual empathy may be invaluable. For example, an older sibling who completely takes over a younger child as a result of poor overall nurturing of all the children can be released from this responsibility. The aims here might be:

(a) rewarding 'required helpfulness', while

(b) encouraging the older child to relinquish elements of the caring role which detract from their own healthy development, and

(c) encouraging age-appropriate initiatives for the older child and assertion in the younger child.

5. Resources available to support parents of children within the community can be vital sources of help, especially for isolated, vulnerable parents. Consideration needs to be given to the parent's current personal resources when making plans for support initiatives. For example, where parents are depressed, making new social links may be very difficult for them, so keeping support initiatives focused and confined helps to minimise the emotional demands on them (Thompson 1995).

6. Ensure that the parents are provided with the financial and material resources that they need to support them in their parenting. This will include ensuring that all due benefits are applied for, that the housing department keeps the house upgraded, that training and job opportunities are available and so on.

7. The search for somewhere permanent to stay for the child, if the living arrangements are uncertain, or if the child has experienced a previous separation, is of vital significance in confirming a sense of a secure base. For the child who is separated from family, it is very important to search for significant family members who may not only be parents or grandparents. For example, even for children who come from families where abuse is endemic, it is often possible to find an extended family member who has survived these difficulties and who can act as a positive role model for the child. Facilitating contact with any important person to the child promotes a sense of continuity and therefore strengthens the sense of secure base.

8. For the child who is at home, it may be that there is an important neighbour who can be encouraged to have consistent nurturing individual contact with the child.

9. Try to organise for continuity of availability of any professionals involved with the child.

10. School can provide an invaluable source of stimulation, care and nourishment and emotional support for vulnerable children. Consideration should be given to the culture which is established within the school, so that it not only welcomes the children in a nurturing fashion, but also is inclusive and respectful towards their parents and extended family members.

11. For children who come from minority ethnic or cultural groups, it is vitally important that the links with their culture remain wherever possible. These links need to be given positive value by those caring for children from different communities if they have to be separated from their birth and extended families. Involvement of the child in familiar religious or cultural events or routines can reassure the child that his or her origins are valued by those caring for them. Such rituals as the preparation of familiar foods give powerful positive messages about the child's culture.

12. Every opportunity needs to be taken with young children in communicating an acceptance of *difference*. This is especially important for children who come from minority social groupings and therefore may already be experiencing prejudice and even rejection. The City of Bradford Metropolitan Council recommends the adoption of techniques with children under 12 who are black or of mixed parentage that can be used in promoting a positive sense of black identity:

    (a) When working in children's homes with 5- and 6-year-olds, who never mention race, it is possible that they have been turned off the subject through overly heavy discussion making them more insecure. The environment may not lend itself to discussions about race. It is important to use natural opportunities to open discussion, when black people are on the TV, in the theatre, in books, or a black issue arises.

    (b) Racial issues should be discussed whenever they come up or as appropriate. If a child reports some incident, activity or statements in which there is a racist element, the racial implications should not be overlooked or diluted. This must be encouraged because these discussions could help the child realise him or herself in terms of society.

(c)   Children in this age group should be exposed as much as possible to black literature and black history. This is the age group in which clarity of thought and the moulding of personality begins.

(d)   Positive black models in the child's environment are essential. It is vital that these models should be selected not only from music and sport, but also from the fields of science, mathematics and medicine in which black people have always made, and are continually making, a contribution.

(e)   For those separated children who come from families where English is not spoken as a first language, it can be of great value to maintain contact with the child's extended family and community. It is also helpful to look for a befriender or mentor who can engage with the child to continue with positive messages about his or her culture.

PRACTICE SUGGESTIONS
EDUCATION

It is essential to work in partnership with the school when making any plans for the improvement of a child's educative experience. As is the case with the other domains, there is much overlap between the area of education and other domains of resilience, for example Social Competencies, Friendships, and so on. Therefore interventions focused on encouraging the child's competence in a school setting often have ripple benefits in other areas of the child's development. The emphasis for vulnerable children needs to be on the planning and preparation for schooling and on the supportive liaison with the school and other professional services.

An approach to school that normalises particular difficulties in learning, helps to identify the learning journey for the individual child and structures the individual steps in learning will encourage parents to be involved in supporting the child.

A whole range of different strategies may be employed to encourage parents' involvement in school and joint strategies for approaching difficulties. Dowling and Osborne (1985) provide many useful ideas for encouraging the positive involvement of the parents in their children's schooling. The book suggests that there are two interrelated tasks in primary schools, first to educate and second to provide care and nurturing. It states that care-giving is an essential part of primary schooling and that without it little or no learning is likely to take place. This emphasis underlines the importance of the key relationship between the child's teacher, the child and parents, especially in the first year of schooling.

Encouraging the child's interest in learning and school

1. Sometimes children find it difficult to understand the point of school and the subjects learned. Pointing out the connections between the different subjects and real-life activities can help to show the importance for example, by finding books about a particular hobby or pop group, writing fan letters, working out football scores, adding up pocket money or clothing grants and working out what to spend it on.

2. There may be many opportunities to model a positive attitude to learning by, for example:

(a)   bringing children books, talking about books

(b)   taking children to libraries and historical places, e.g. castles, child-oriented museums, bookshops

(c)   exploring the use of CD-ROMs and the internet

(d)   playing cards, darts and board games involving counting

(e)   letting them help work out mileage claims

(f)   encouraging them to use the local A–Z of street maps or road maps when driving to places.

3.   An emphasis in the school setting on celebration of even minor achievements, for example, putting up individual children's pictures around the classroom and school corridors can be an important message of valuing the individual child. Involvement of the individual child in special tasks or responsibilities can promote self-esteem, for example being responsible for the class pet hamster or for the provision of necessary equipment for the school peer group.

4.   After-school activities (for example homework clubs) that encourage the completion of homework can also be helpful in establishing a culture of the enjoyment of learning and a completion of tasks.

5.   Some children develop a school phobia that can be triggered by the sight, smells, sounds and so on of the school building. Even if the original reason for anxiety has been removed (for example bullying) the child may still feel fear of school. An educational psychologist will be able to provide a programme to help overcome the phobia.

6.   Lack of concentration is a very common problem for children who have been abused or neglected. It is very undermining of learning, and can be associated with the child becoming disruptive to others in the class when bored. Children can learn to concentrate, but need the patient attention of a supportive adult, perhaps a classroom assistant to help them through the points at which they habitually give up on a task. The Social Competence domain also contains suggestions of activities to help with concentration.

7.   It can be helpful to structure simple, annual personal profiles of the individual child in order to identify needs and strengths. Building on the child's particular interest or achievement within the class timetable can be encouraged in primary school settings.

8. Some children will need extra support in the primary school setting over and above informal supports of the kind already suggested. Early identification of the individual needs of children can help in anticipating the child's need for such support so that the 'scaffolding' already suggested can be more effective in pacing the learning to the particular child's individual needs. Effective multidisciplinary assessments can be especially valuable here.

9. Although the child might adopt an attitude of not caring about school he or she is likely to feel keenly a sense of exclusion from 'normal' school activities and progress. Anything positive that the child can be encouraged to identify about the school as a place, education as a process or teachers as people can be used as a bridge back into schooling.

10. Encourage the child's involvement in school trips and special activities, as well as holiday play schemes to enhance the child's involvement with his or her peer group and help in the identification of special interests or skills.

Encouraging a parent or carer environment that facilitates the child's learning and school attendance

1. The ways in which schools involve parents and carers in assessing, monitoring and building the child's capacities for learning are modelled in every school communication with home. Some parents will need help in making and sustaining this link and this can be modelled by supportive professionals. Parents can be involved in the school setting in a number of ways, for example as helpers on school trips, or at break times and this can be very important in building the key relationships which will sustain the vulnerable child in the school setting. It can also have the secondary benefit of encouraging parents' confidence in communicating effectively with adults at school and therefore feeling more a part of their child's education.

2. Initiatives taken to involve parents at an early stage can offer them ideas as to how they might encourage the child's school achievement by the use of games and play ideas at home. The transition from nursery into primary school is a key developmental hurdle and this can be eased by

the deliberate involvement of parents with their children in the entry and early settling into formal schooling.

3. Provide opportunities for parents to have access to learning materials that are being used with their children to enable them to keep track of their child's progress.

4. If the family is living in overcrowded or poor housing conditions then it may be very difficult for the child to find space and peace in which to do homework. This issue can form part of a case to housing departments for a move to more suitable housing. In the mean time it may be helpful to see if anyone else in the extended family can offer the child a peaceful space in which to work.

5. Look for somebody in the extended family or neighbourhood who could act as a homework mentor.

6. It may be necessary to set up regular meetings to monitor the child's early progress in a school setting, not only for those children who have established behaviour problems and who are therefore vulnerable to potential school failure, but also for those children who may be experiencing difficulties in separating from their attachment figures. Encouragement of parents to attend parents' evenings and events within the school may need particular emphasis for parents who are reluctant to enter school settings. Through this simple mechanism parents can not only establish a relationship with the individual teacher, but also gain an understanding of the patterns of formal learning which their child is experiencing. Modelling parents' involvement in the school through support of the professionals involved can be helpful in establishing good communication and relationships with school staff. This should occur even if the child is not living at home.

7. Parents of children who have identified special needs may need particular encouragement to be involved in supporting their child's schooling, bearing in mind the likelihood that many parents have had negative experiences of education.

8. There should be an assessment of the parents' own educational needs. Helping the parents to further their own education will not only be of benefit to them but will have knock-on benefits for their children. Community education and adult education organisations provide a variety of options of classes for adults.

Exploring opportunities in the wider environment to support this child's education

1. Ordinary community activities, such as Brownies or Guides, Scouts and swimming clubs, can offer very important opportunities for children who may be otherwise more isolated from their peer group in school. They can, furthermore, be particularly helpful for accommodated children who may feel themselves set apart from their peers as their living circumstances are at odds with the family context of their classmates. The regular involvement of children in local community clubs can, therefore, build a sense of social connectedness with the child's peer group in the local community and begin to develop a sense of belonging.

2. If there is a particular teacher with whom the child has developed a relationship of trust, then this teacher should be involved in planning meetings.

3. It can be useful, especially in work with vulnerable young children entering school, to identify a mentor to assist in getting a young child to school and supporting them through the day. Primary school settings are often helpful in this regard in that there are often supportive adults other than the main class teacher who can keep an eye on the vulnerable child.

4. Numerous initiatives have been generated by local communities in order to support children in primary school settings. For example, groups of adults from particular racial groupings have become concerned about the number of children from their own communities who appear not to be reaching their potential at school. Initiatives such as the individual linking of these supportive adults in the community with individual children to support school progress can be profoundly helpful.

5. A buddy or mentoring system involving older pupils looking after younger pupils can often be available in primary schools or can be suggested by parents or professionals.

6. Some children may benefit particularly from involvement in breakfast clubs and/or in lunch clubs and out-of-school activities.

7. Many activity-based groups within the community can provide school-aged children with opportunities for mastery and success in

particular areas. For example, local groups which nurture children's footballing or gymnastic skills can help with developing the child's feeling of competence and these benefits can spill over into confidence in a school setting, particularly when these activities are undertaken with school peers. Shared activities in such a group can also build social competence, developing empathy and responsiveness towards peers. The more involved the child can be in community activities which surround the school or which may feed into the child's ability to cope in school the better. For example, community projects, celebrations or environmental initiatives can foster a sense of social responsibility and a sense of belonging to the school community.

PRACTICE SUGGESTIONS
FRIENDSHIPS

With this domain and this age group it is clear that it is school that offers the greatest potential as a site for intervention. As has been explored in the domain of Education, school offers a whole range of sources for the boosting of resilience, and peer relationships are at the heart of many of these. When considering intervention within this domain it may be helpful to consider general peer relationships and specific friendships. It may be that a child needs help with general peer relationships first before attention to particular friendships. Another child might have many general acquaintances but no special friends. The starting point has to be the child's perception of the situation: however many friends he or she may objectively appear to have, a child can still feel lonely and it is that feeling that is important. So, before planning intervention take care to locate the root problem that is affecting friendships.

Helping the child to develop the characteristics that help with making and keeping friends

1. If the child appears to have problems with peer relationships in general then he or she may need help with social skills, as set out in the domain of Social Competencies. Modelling can work, for example, one successful method is showing a child a film of an

initially withdrawn child engaged in increasingly complex peer interactions.

2. Use role play, cartoons, drawings and so on to encourage him or her to rehearse and practise skills such as joining a group, managing teasing, playing cooperatively and so on.

3. There may be strengths in other domains that can be used to help build upon this domain. For example, if the child has a particular talent or interest he or she can be enrolled in a club or interest group not only in order to develop that talent, but also to enable contact with children who have similar interests. He or she can also be encouraged to pass expertise on to other children, perhaps as part of a mentor scheme. If the child is strong in the domain of academic performance he or she could be brought into a peer tutoring scheme.

4. If the child has difficulty with identifying special friends then spend time with him or her exploring what kind of things children can enjoy doing together, for example some games cannot be played alone. It might be helpful to suggest that different friendships can be encouraged for different activities. For example, can he or she think of a classmate to play computer games with, another to work on a school project with, another to go to a club with and so on.

5. If the child describes friendships only on the basis of proximity, then help him or her to think about friendships as sources of support and shared confidences.

6. If the child is lacking in self-confidence and self-esteem he or she may not see him or herself as having anything to offer as a friend. Try generating a list of the child's characteristics and presenting them as qualities of friendship. Even less obvious characteristics can be seen as assets, for example, the shy and quiet child can offer a good listening ear, the noisy child can speak up for a friend, the risk-taking child can be a friend who encourages a timid friend to try a new sport or activity.

Encouraging a parent or carer environment that facilitates the development of friendship

1. Many children have home circumstances that make it very difficult for them to invite other children around. For example, some households are embarrassingly chaotic or untidy. If there is a parent who misuses

alcohol or drugs his or her reaction towards friends can be unpredictable. A child who is being sexually abused by a father or father figure may want to protect a friend from similar abuse. If the child does have such difficulties then help him or her to generate strategies to manage friendships. Perhaps a grandparent or other relative will be happy to act as a base for getting together. He or she might need help with developing reasonable explanations for why they would prefer to go to their friend's house. In some situations, with parental permission and care, a friend's parent could be involved in discussions about how to support the friendship.

2.   Children who are referred because of neglect often have parents who are isolated and lack friends. Because young children are highly dependent upon their parents for contact with other children, the knock-on effect of parental isolation is restricted contact with peers. Parents of neglected children also have a tendency to perceive themselves as more lonely and lacking in support, perhaps because of low self-esteem and self-efficacy. Therefore, intervention may need to focus upon helping the parent to make more satisfactory friendships themselves.

3.   If parents do not have the time, energy, resources or will to help children make arrangements with friends then what might help? For example, perhaps all the child's friends have mobile phones: could the family and extended family be encouraged to pay the child for some chores so that he or she can save up for one of their own? Parents might need information and advice about the importance of their role in friendships. Can a father be encouraged to help out, even if he does not live in the same household?

4.   Younger children's play with other children is frequently in the presence of adults who can intervene as problems occur. Older children whose emotional development is immature may need a similar level of close supervision from a parent or carer. The parent may benefit from advice on how to mediate disputes.

Helping with the child's current friendships

1.   If the child is mainly engaged in solitary play he or she may need help in group play.

2.   If the child identifies a particular friend then assess how best to support and encourage the

friendship, perhaps by arranging joint activities. The friendship might seem to be unhelpful, in which case try to arrange for the child to be in close proximity with other children.

3. Interacting with another child involves a number of skills (Dodge *et al.* 1986):

    (a) Working out accurately what the other child is doing (for example, waving an arm at you).

    (b) Interpreting the information properly (the child is waving a greeting, not gesturing for you to go away).

    (c) Searching for an appropriate responses (waving back, shouting abuse, asking to join in, ignoring them).

    (d) Choosing the best response (waving back and then asking to join in).

    (e) Carrying out the chosen response.

    Children who are rejected by their peers seem to misinterpret other children's behaviour, for example, seeing a friendly overture as hostile, and also have a tendency to be more likely to chose an aggressive response. With role play, group work, discussion and reflection children can be taught to stop and think about alternative interpretations of behaviour and less aggressive responses (see also Social Competencies domain). Of course, the other child might have been gesturing for him or her to go away because consistently aggressive children are likely to elicit more negative responses. You may need to arrange for the child to take part in structured, supervised peer group activity.

4. It is asking a lot of a developmentally immature child to expect them to sustain friendships with children who do not live near them. The challenge is to contrive ways of placing children in proximity with children without difficulties. School is the obvious setting for this. Look also at all possible local community resources. It may be that there is a local youth project that does not have the resources to take challenging children. Rather than referring to a specialist project explore ways in which the local authority can work in partnership with the local group to enable it to cater for children with difficulties.

5. In their review of peer relations, Malik and Furman (1993) describe approaches to helping with peer problems including:

(a) *Social skills training with individuals or groups to help with difficulties with interpersonal interactions.* Some commercial programmes teach social skills, for example listening, handling 'saying no' to avoid trouble in a series of lessons. These programmes seem to work best with children aged 10 or under. Skills are broken down into components, explained to the child and role play is used to practise skills.

(b) *Social cognitive training to help with underlying cognitive processes that affect overt behaviour.* For example, one programme teaches children effective problem-solving style and impulse control. Children are taught to ask themselves four questions:

   (i)   What is my problem?

   (ii) How can I solve it?

   (iii) Am I using the best plan?

   (iv) How did I do it?

(c) *Fostering successful peer experiences which helps children in unsupervised peer group activity.* Children start in highly structured therapy group to learn social skills, then participate in a highly structured naturalistic peer group like swimming lessons, then in a pairs interaction with adult supervision, then a naturalistic peer group of 'intermediate difficulty', e.g. outdoor activities and finally they join a naturally occurring semi-structured group like scouts or sports groups.

(d) *Changing social contexts where the social context is made more conducive to good peer relations.* An example of this is the instigation of anti-bullying policies in schools.

PRACTICE SUGGESTIONS
TALENTS AND INTERESTS

It should be remembered that in considering the benefits *across* domains, talents and interests, especially those that bring them into contact with supportive adults and peers, can help the child to settle within a new community and school setting.

If there is already an area of strength it will be important to capitalise on established skills. However, in the work with many children, established talents and abilities may not be readily apparent in the work and intervention should focus on how the child's potential abilities can be explored.

The case studies at the end of this workbook illustrate the potential for using an ability or talent to support a healthy sense of identity in a child who has experienced not only abuse, but also many separations and losses. It will be seen from the examples that some children and young people who avoid intimacy with caring adults, or who are ambivalent, can experience the support of adults over time in developing a set of talents. This, less obviously than in direct attempts to bring the child to accept caring overtures, can build the child's ability to depend healthily on those caring for him or her.

Therefore, this domain links closely with the notion of the child being able to say 'I can' in relation to his or her own capacities. It also helps to build a sense of identity in exploring and establishing, not only competencies, but also a sense of identity rooted in a unique collection of attributes. In this way, the ' I can' contributes to the 'I am' or what can be seen as self-esteem.

Encouraging the child in his or her particular talents and interests

1. Some school-aged children have no idea even what activities they wish to try. A stalwart carer, parent or relative can be invaluable in persisting and trying out a whole range of different activities.

2. Some children with disabilities can excel in particular areas and may need persistent interest by at least one caring adult to discover and then support the talent or ability. This can begin to build a healthier sense of identity for a child with disability. For example, Derek has profound learning difficulties; however, he is a very expressive boy and has learned to use simple play figures to act out dramas and imaginative play. He recently chose this medium to begin to express some confusions and distress about the circumstances of his removal from home. His social worker and foster carer were able to harness this natural expressive ability in detailed emotional work on his life story.

3. A talent can give a child a vehicle for expressing feelings, for example:

   (a) cartoon drawing

    (b)   computer skills

    (c)   design or artistic skills.

4.   A great deal of persistence may be required in finding a particular talent or ability in an individual child. Because many children have a natural lack of confidence, particularly if they have been ignored or discouraged, great tenacity can be required to communicate the belief in the child's ability by maintaining effort, even in the face of the child's passivity and apparent diffidence.

5.   Physical activities have the positive benefit of providing a natural discharge of tension and anxiety. This can help the child to develop an awareness of his or her body and promote a sense of well-being. For example Mary, who was 13 and had a natural ability in running, needed the support of her coach to pace herself physically in order to make the most of her performance.

6.   Confidence in a talent may allow the child for the first time to begin to acknowledge fears about failures or gaps in knowledge, especially for a child who is naturally defensive in his or her attitude.

7.   At this stage new developmental capacities become apparent which can be harnessed in the enjoyment of a talent or interest and can be used to help children value their skills for example, the ability to memorise details of a favourite sport team's scoring and progress through a league. This new capacity for memory can be developed and extended through the memorising of a dance or dance routine or songs. Similarly, the child can be encouraged to develop rational thinking, specifically linked between cause and effect, for example:

> 'If I foul another player I will get sent off.'

> 'If I practise hard I will be appreciated and succeed.'

The key here is to select natural enthusiasm in the child and link it deliberately with other skills and domains.

8.   A child's talent can be deliberately recognised and celebrated in school, thereby encouraging the linking of the enthusiasm of the talent with other skills, for example writing about his or her talent or hobby, drawing a particular incident, giving a small talk to other children in class.

Ensuring that the parent or carer environment supports the development of talents and interests

1. There is a real opportunity for adults to learn from the child in a particular area:

    (a) Teach me that dance.

    (b) Teach me that magic trick.

    (c) Show me how to make that kite.

    (d) Help me work the computer.

    This can be a tremendous boost to the child's self-esteem.

2. Involvement in a favourite hobby or talent may be a useful focus for meaningful involvement of fathers with their children, including those in circumstances of marital or partner separation.

3. Separated children can still share enjoyable times with parents or relatives through shared activities that build a sense of family connection as well as individual competence. For example, Steven loves golf and his mother takes him to the driving range near to the foster carers when she visits. She collects pictures of his golfing heroes and the social worker has supported her by paying for basic lessons for Steven that his mother takes him to each week. Sarah's grandfather takes her to the home games of their local football team. He recently went to see her play in the school mixed team.

4. Some children choose precisely the activity for which they are not obviously equipped, but this should not stop them taking part. For example, Shona particularly wanted to be good at gymnastics. Her coordination skills were poor, however, and her carers feared she would face disappointment. Through a close, cooperative link with the teacher in the local gymnastic class, her carers at first became helpers supporting her to attend regularly. Because they developed a knowledge of the exercises, they were then able to help her to practise at home and she soon surpassed their expectations, such was her determination. This interest provided a shared activity that was powerful in building her gradual attachment to her carers.

5. Parents may need support to believe in their own abilities to help their child to develop a talent or a skill. For example, if they have had poor experiences of play in their own childhood they may be at a loss as to how to create opportunities for play for their child. It may well be

constructive to support parents individually or in groups to enjoy play opportunities for themselves and to rediscover or find out for the first time their own skills and capacities.

6. Working with parents' own talents, abilities and strengths has many advantages as it models confidence and enjoyment for the child. For example, Kelly's mother, Susan, rediscovered her dance skills through going to a local dance class and realised she could teach her daughter, who also has a natural ability. Mother and daughter now regularly attend classes together, an activity that they both enjoy.

Drawing upon opportunities in the wider community to nurture the child's talents and interests

1. It is helpful to remember that some children need more assistance than others at this stage to take part in a shared group activity involving a skill or an ability. Billy, who tended to lash out when frustrated, needed the support of his uncle to sustain attendance at the football club. His uncle's involvement in the club and regular encouragement made it possible for Billy to sustain an activity for the first time. Paula's adolescent foster sister, Laura, is a medal and cup winner in the drum majorettes; Paula loves to go to the sessions with Laura and in fact won her own first medal recently. Tom has an interest and ability in modern dance but is teased about this at school. His male foster carer actively supports him and encourages him to practise at home. His achievements are celebrated in the foster home with photographs, videos and certificates that have been framed by the carers and are on the walls in the sitting room.

2. A talent or hobby can offer a link with a different group of peers, thereby opening up social networks for accommodated young people, for example:

   (a) joining a drama group in the local community

   (b) exploring a musical interest by joining a group either in the community or from a school base.

3. Shared interests at this age and stage can form a common basis of friendship either in school or in an interest group in the community, for example Brownies or Guides, Venture Scouts, football, darts and so on.

This can be all the more important if the interest is a solitary one, such as computing.

4. If a child is placed in accommodation with others with similar problems it can change the emphasis of some aspects of the child's social experience to place them in an activity with more able peers in other community settings.

5. Make supportive adults available who may act as a mentor for the child, a relationship that can last through into adolescence. Children from minority cultures can find a secure base in activities linked with their own cultural heritage, for example dance or key position in religious observance to rituals. Finding an adult to act as a mentor from the child's natural networks in the community is particularly important here.

PRACTICE SUGGESTIONS
POSITIVE VALUES

Helping this child develop moral reasoning and to understand his or her own feelings and empathise with those of people close to them

1. Some children whose emotional life has been very deprived may be operating at a much younger level in this domain. You may want to draw on suggestions from the *Early Years* workbook in these cases.

2. A technique of using 'dilemma discussion groups' has been shown to be a successful way to raise a child's level of moral reasoning (Goldstein 1999). A full description of the technique is beyond the scope of these workbooks; however, the principles could be applied to a range of group settings, perhaps using the dilemma provided. Briefly, the technique involves holding discussions with a group of children operating at different

levels of moral reasoning. The group leaders should be familiar with the different levels of reasoning. Their role is to encourage the children to explain the underlying reasoning for their responses to different moral dilemmas, preferably as real to life as possible. They then encourage debate among children at different levels. The leaders do not express a view as to what is the right or wrong answer, but aim to provide an environment of openness and trust in which children can themselves work out what is 'good'.

3. Real situations in which the child has been in trouble can be used as a basis for a discussion in which the focus in mainly upon the *reasoning* behind an action. If a child has been caught stealing, for example, he or she can be asked questions such as:

    (a) What if everybody stole what they wanted?

    (b) What if no one stole things?

    (c) What if your best friend took something of yours?

    (d) What if someone you don't like took something of yours?

    (e) How do you think people can get things without stealing?, and so on.

4. If the child appears to have a difficulty with understanding about intention, then some time can be spent with them exploring the difference between accidental and deliberate harm. Parents and carers can be encouraged to stress the difference during ordinary day-to-day activities. The school teacher can be vital here as there are many opportunities during the school day to point out the difference between accidents and intention.

5. It may be that some children are routinely punished for accidental incidents and in these cases work directly with the parents to help them with appreciation of the difference between accidental and deliberate actions. Sometimes parents lack sufficient information about what can be reasonably expected from children at different ages and parenting classes could help in these cases.

6. The activities described for early years children might be applicable for some younger school-age children who show problems with empathy (see *Early Years* workbook).

7. It is through relationships with others that children begin to develop an understanding of their own and others' feelings. Ensure that there is at

least one person in the child's life who has the interest and the time to listen to him or her, explore feelings and demonstrate respect and empathy for the child.

8. Feschbach (1984) devised and tested an empathy training programme for implementation within schools. The programme was devised to help children:

    (a) identify another's emotional state

    (b) take another's perspective

    (c) experience in themselves the emotions of others.

    Thirty hours of exercises were planned for use in small groups of four to six children over a series of sessions. The following is an extract from the description of the programme:

    > To increase skill in affect identification, children were asked to identify the emotions conveyed in photographs of facial expressions, tape-recordings of affect-laden conversations, and videotaped pantomimes of emotional situations. In addition, the children themselves role played in a wide range of games and situations in which they acted out and guessed feelings. To foster children's ability to assume the perspective of another person, training exercises include a variety of games and activities that become progressively more difficult as training proceeds. Early in the training program, the children were asked to experience and imagine various visual perspectives ('What would the world look like to you if you were…as small as a cat?'). They were asked to imagine the preferences and behaviour of different kinds of people ('What birthday present would make each member of your family happiest?'…). Children listened to stories, then recounted them from the point of view of each character in the story. Numerous later sessions were devoted to role playing. In these role-playing sessions children were given the opportunity to play a part in a scene, then to switch roles and play the parts of other characters, thus experiencing several perspectives on the same interaction. For other activities children viewed videotapes of their enactments to enable them to gain an outside perspective of themselves and the situations enacted. Discussions followed role-playing sessions and included identification of the feelings experienced by the characters enacted. (Fesbach 1984, p.197)

Encouraging the child to help others

1. The parent or carer should be encouraged to recognise, accept and praise any verbal offers of help or apparent attempts to help. School-age children can be expected to help in ways that are actually useful in the home. Rather than expecting the child to help just whenever asked, it may be more straightforward to spend some time with the child and parent devising a simple set of chores that are carried out at regular times. If necessary a reward system can be built into the plan.

2. Because of their extensive experience of child care, many foster parents will want to ask children to help with chores. There may be anxieties about how much is appropriate, especially if a child has been expected to carry out too much work at home. The appropriate amount of required helpfulness can be discussed in planning discussions so that all involved can agree on a level.

3. When there is no appropriate support for a child's helping behaviour in the home, and the likelihood of this changing is minimal, then look for other people in the child's network who appear to have the patience to help, for example, grandparents could be encouraged to ask the child to help them with shopping, tidying up, weeding, cleaning the car, washing up and so on. Again, a regular arrangement is likely to be more effective.

Encouraging the child to show comforting, sharing and more general prosocial behaviour

1. The ideal way for children to learn positive behaviour is by imitation. All interactions with the child should therefore model caring and comforting. Again the parent or carer has to be the main resource here. Parents may need advice and support to actively encourage  comforting and sharing behaviour between siblings and the child and other children.

2. Children should be given clear rules and boundaries about behaviour towards others and any signs of cruelty, unkindness or hurting to other children or adults should be stopped.

131

3. Any spontaneous act of sharing or kindness should be praised and reinforced. Parents may need advice on how best to do this.

4. Contact with pets and animals can help with the development of kindness. If it is not appropriate for there to be a pet in the household, there may be opportunities for children to help with a relative or neighbour's pet. Older children can be encouraged to offer to walk a neighbour's dog, for example. Trips to city farms or zoos with pets' corners that allow animal handling may also help.

5. If a child is showing active signs of cruelty to others then his or her behaviour will require a high level of monitoring by skilled staff who can intervene as quickly as possible with firm and clear messages against harm to others. All in the child's network need to work together to give consistent and clear messages about kindness to others.

6. Children need to have contact with their peers in order to learn about cooperative activities. School is an obvious place for the encouragement of cooperation. Ensure that the child has access to some form of formal or informal contact with other children that is supervised by an adult skilled in facilitating cooperative activities. Children can be referred to one of the many group work programmes set up to involve a range of activities that require cooperation. When involving children in group work take time before they join the group to discuss the values of the group with them so that they are prepared for, and understand, the requirements of mutual respect, confidentiality and so on.

7. Children live up to the attributions ascribed to them, so whenever appropriate they need to hear that they are good and kind: 'That was kind of you to...'

8. Find community-based schemes that promote responsibility and empathy, for example, local clean-up river campaigns, anti-litter drives, sponsored walks, charity collections and so on. Wherever possible involve the child in mainstream community activities.

9. Older children can be involved in buddying schemes with younger children, to help them with schoolwork, or with other activities of mutual interest.

PRACTICE SUGGESTIONS
SOCIAL COMPETENCIES

 A considerable number of resources are available to help with the promotion of social competencies in school-age children, many of them designed for use in schools. The 'Promoting Social Competence' project has compiled a database of such resources (Promoting Social Competence 1999).

Some examples of programmes that might be helpful are described below.

Peterson and Gannoni's *Stop Think Do* which uses traffic light symbols as a motif within a range of activities aimed at encouraging children and young people to stop and think of options rather than acting on impulse (Peterson and Gannoni 1992).

Kreidler's *Creative Conflict Resolution* contains more than 200 simple activities aimed at teaching children strategies for dealing with problems in social interaction. Designed primarily for classroom use, many of the activities could be adapted for use in other group settings, or on a one-to-one basis (Kreidler 1984).

Spence's *Social Skills Training* is again designed for use in schools, but contains a range of questionnaires and checklists for children and teachers on problems of social situations, social skills and so on. There is a photocopiable resource book that has paper-and-pencil task sheets to help children consider alternative ways of responding (Spence 1995).

Goldstein's *Prepare Curriculum* describes a whole range of activities for teaching prosocial and social competence skills. It sets out the research base for different approaches and gives detailed descriptions of individual and group programmes (Goldstein 1999).

Before looking at suggestions for each of the aspects, we will set out an overall framework for considering social competence problems.

Smith and Carlson (1997) have brought together much useful information about children's coping with stress. In summary, they describe coping as involving four steps:

1. Appraisal of the meaning of the event, whether it is stressful and whether it might be controllable.

2. Selecting a coping strategy that is appropriate to the circumstances.

3. Carrying out the coping strategy.

4. Evaluating whether the coping strategy has been successful.

Some stressful situations are malleable and to some extent controllable. Other stressors are uncontrollable. When stressors are malleable it is better to use the active (or 'primary') problem-focused coping strategies such as gaining information or actually changing the stressor. When the situation is uncontrollable then it is better to use the passive (or 'secondary') emotion-focused strategies such as changing the way you think about the stressor or adapting to it. Therefore the accuracy of attributions made about events can affect choice of coping strategy and the likelihood of success. Put simply the choice is between changing the events or changing how you think and feel about the events.

School-age children have been shown to have the capacity to use both problem-focused and emotion-focused coping strategies. However, a range of factors can influence the choice and success of coping strategy. To use a problem-focused strategy children must believe that they can have an impact on the stressor; they need a good sense of self-efficacy. They also need problem-solving skills and the social skills to enlist social support. Economic resources can help 'buy' the emotion-focused strategies of distraction, such as entertainment.

The key to developing effective intervention then is to assess accurately where the child's problem with social competence lies in the chain of coping as shown in Figure 9.1.

APPRAISAL

Is this event likely to be stressful?

(Requires ability to assess whether an event is likely to affect well-being)

↓

Is this event in any way under my control?

(Requires accurate attributions and self-efficacy)

↓

CHOICE OF COPING STRATEGY

What can I do about this event?

(Requires a range of strategies and ability to match strategy to problem)

↙　　　　　　　　　　↘

PROBLEM-FOCUSED　　　　　**EMOTION-FOCUSED**

Have I strategies I can use?　　　　Can I change the way I
(Requires coping resources such as　　think about this event?
problem-solving skills)　　　　(Requires self-efficacy and self-esteem)

Can I put these strategies into action?　　Can I change the way I
(Requires self-efficacy and self-esteem)　　feel about this event?
　　　　　　　　　　(Requires emotional support, family or
　　　　　　　　　　social support)

↓

CARRYING OUT THE STRATEGY

(Requires confidence, courage and expectation of success)

↓

EVALUATING THE STRATEGY

(Requires ability to reflect and learn from experience)

Figure 9.1 The chain of coping that enables successful social competence

For example, a child who lacks social competence may not play with other children because she consistently wrongly appraises the approach of other children as threatening. She needs to learn strategies of assessing who is approaching her, paying attention to the facial expressions, listening to what the child is saying and so on.

Another child might accurately appraise the approach of another child as friendly, but finds it stressful because he does not feel that he has the interpersonal skills to respond properly, he feels shy or tongue-tied and that he has no control over the situation. He needs to learn simple strategies of greeting and engaging with others. Role play can be an ideal way to teach a child such skills and thereby to boost self-efficacy.

Another child might choose emotion-led strategies such as thinking 'I don't need friends', 'I don't care if I get into a fight', 'I don't like her so it doesn't matter if she is unfriendly'. She might also benefit from learning more problem-focused strategies of how to respond to other children.

Another child might consistently refuse to do the work the teacher asks him to do and end up being punished frequently. This could be a coping strategy of avoiding the feeling of failure if he fails at the work. What he does not realise is that his strategy is not effective. He might benefit from looking at the outcome (getting punished) and thinking of other options, for example, asking for help with the work.

Helping the child to develop the personal characteristics that help with social competence

AUTONOMY

Children who lack social competence may have their autonomy curtailed by adults trying to keep them out of trouble. The downside to this is that their opportunities to learn from experience are reduced. Explore ways in which they can safely experience autonomy. These could include:

- arranging for him or her to make their own way to a destination, but checking that they have arrived

- involving him or her in all decision-making processes as far as possible

- seeking his or her opinion on matters affecting him or her

- ensuring that he or she has access to some money of their own to spend as he or she wishes

- supporting him or her to make an arrangement to meet with a friend

- giving him or her small responsibilities and gradually building them up.

SELF-CONTROL/PROBLEM-SOLVING

Children need to learn a range of problem-solving skills if they are to engage in problem-focused coping strategies for social situations. In the commercially existing programmes for teaching social competencies a number of themes and techniques emerge that can be adapted:

1. Teaching children to stop and think before acting – thinking can be encouraged in discussion, in groups or by using written vignettes that the child is asked to consider.

2. Demonstrating alternative ways of reacting and then encouraging role play of situations that are directly relevant to the child.

3. Taking a problem situation and helping the child to identify the *thoughts* and *feelings* that the situation evoked. Looking at the links between the thoughts and feelings, and helping the child to replace the thoughts with different thoughts. For example, when asked to read out in class the child thinks 'Everyone will look at me and will think I am stupid' and consequently feels scared. Instead the child could think 'Any one of us could be asked to read aloud, they all know what it's like, they'll feel sorry for me'.

4. Group-based cognitive-behavioural programmes are effective for teaching interaction with friends, sensitivity to others and resisting peer pressure, as well as the skills of communicating clearly, problem-solving and self-control (Smith and Carlson 1997).

5. Helping children reflect and understand the event and their behaviour (and the behaviour of others).

6. Brainstorming a range of solutions with children.

7. Providing children with information about a situation and encouraging them to carry out their own 'risk assessment' for different choices of action.

8. Helping children take time out and reflect in a way that is safe.

9. Helping children to make links between cause and effect.

TEMPERAMENT

There is evidence that differences in temperament can be exhibited at a very young age (Buss and Plomin 1984; Chess and Thomas 1977) and having a positive easy temperament is a major factor in promoting resilience. For a child with a less easy temperament the most effective care is that which meshes with the child. If a parent withdraws from a difficult child and is critical, then the child is likely to become even more difficult. The parent or carer should be encouraged to continue to show affection for the child, while dealing with the problem behaviour (Santrok 1994). If looking for alternative full-time carers or mentors, then attention has to be paid to the 'fit' between adult and child temperament.

SELF-EFFICACY

Children who have been neglected or abused frequently develop attributions for events as out of their control, likely to remain negative and as being global. This can make them very reluctant to try new tasks, because they believe that they will fail. The experience of positive events, such as an enjoyable outing, the concentrated attention of a liked adult and so on, can help to change this view that good things will not happen to them.

1. The child has to be encouraged to try simple tasks at which he or she can succeed. This requires skill on behalf of the helper to manipulate situations so that the child tries something almost before realising it. Mentors and teachers can help with this.

2. The child also then needs to learn that some tasks are not within his or her range and that this is not their fault. School is the obvious place to do such work. In conjunction with a teacher a plan could focus on taking the time to help the child understand the difference between problems that can be worked out with effort and problems that he or she would not be expected to solve. Textbooks aimed at older children could be used to demonstrate this. Adults can also model the fact that there are some tasks that are beyond them.

ATTENTION

It is essential that school-aged children know how to direct their attention in academic and social situations. Try to find a member of the child's network who is prepared to spend some concentrated time with the child on a regular occasion. An older pupil at school might be able to be a mentor. A number of activities can be suggested:

1. Encourage and reward the child for looking at you when you talk to him or her.

2. Engage the child's attention and talk to him or her about things that interest him or her, all the while praising him or her for listening.

3. Find a game he or she likes and play it regularly, increasing the length of time you encourage him or her to play each time and praising the child.

4. Use videos with very short stories or cartoons, and move on to increasingly longer videos, watch them with the child and engage in joint attention to details.

5. Find very short stories to read right through and make coming to the end an exciting occasion. If he or she needs a break, pick up where you left off and continue to the end.

6. Use drawing, writing, computer games, CD-ROMs and other activities to encourage concentration.

7. Use stories to help children attend to cause and effect.

8. Make sure that you listen to things the child tries to tell you, show that you are interested in hearing what they have to say, ask them further questions about what they are telling you, draw other members of the family into the conversation.

9. Ensure that schoolwork tasks are broken down into manageable chunks, and gradually increase the size of the chunks.

Helping the parent or carer to provide an environment that encourages social competence

1. The most successful social competence interventions focus on all ecological levels. As well as helping the child to learn social skills and to develop self-efficacy, intervention should aim to create a home environment that fosters good interpersonal skills (Masten and Coatsworth 1998). Work with the parent or carer to devise a list of social competencies that they would like to see their child develop. Help them to develop strategies, based upon reward, for

their encouragement. For example, praise for responding quickly when spoken to or for saying please and thank you, pocket money for a reduction in aggression.

2. Authoritative parenting incorporates both warmth and consistent boundaries. Parents may well benefit from the opportunity to attend a parenting group where they can share their experiences with others and consider different ways of encouraging social competence in their children. When parents themselves lack social competence and perhaps condone their children's behaviour, then look for an alternative role model for the child, for example a member of the extended family, a mentor, volunteer, keyworker, teacher and so on.

Helping the child to develop competence in a wider social environment

1. Ensure that the child has access to and knows how to make use of social support, either informal (friends, extended family) or formal (mentors, social workers, teachers, club leaders).

2. Encourage the community to provide and staff safe play areas or youth clubs for children.

3. Make use of after-school clubs.

4. Encourage social interaction and open communication in a warm and accepting environment.

5. Model conflict resolution for example by calling family conferences.

6. Involve the child in reviews and meetings, involve the child in setting the agenda, choosing the venue for pieces of work and so on. Meaningful rather than token involvement might require 'coaching' the child in techniques for communicating in formal meetings.

7. Encourage and facilitate the child to participate in drawing up rules and sanctions in a number of different settings.

8. Refer to appropriate group work programmes, preferably within mainstream settings.

9. Make sure children know they have choices.

10

Case Studies

PAULA, AGED 7

Vulnerabilities and adversities

Paula was placed with her adoptive parents, aged 7, with a history of parental neglect. She was a child who had 'parented' herself and had taken a caring role for her mother. The worker who placed Paula was concerned about her lack of attachment and the future of the placement. Paula was struggling with her schoolwork and staff were questioning the suitability of her placement there. She had direct contact with her birth mother that occurred frequently, reinforced her parental role and rekindled conflicts of loyalty.

Intervention

SECURE BASE

Paula had committed adoptive parents. She had a tender relationship with their son. The adopters had a support worker who trusted their judgement and helped them to persist in ordinary but powerful initiation towards Paula. Contact with birth mother was reduced and supervised.

EDUCATION

A teacher at school took a real interest in Paula, who struggled with basic learning. She confided a passionate wish to catch up enough not to stand out in class and her teachers and carers formed a strong alliance to offer her extra support. Her male carer helped her each night with homework and she very gradually learned to risk trusting him.

FRIENDSHIPS

Paula found it hard to make friends but has gradually made a strong link with a girl in her gym club. She has needed her female carer's support to establish and maintain this link as she has a tendency to dominate other children, such was her desperation for a friend. Gradually Paula is turning toward her carers through their committed support of her wishes and interests.

TALENTS AND INTERESTS

Paula had few obvious talents but harboured a strong wish to be good at gymnastics. Her physical coordination was poor and this seemed a most unlikely area for success. Nevertheless, her carers took her interest seriously and helped her join a gym class after school and supported her in practising for many hours at home.

Messages

The carers were despondent about Paula's ability to get close to them. The more they tried, the more anxious and avoidant she became. While Paula's worker was at first concerned that they were spending too much time on homework and activities outwith the home, he now sees this bearing fruit in Paula's reliance on the family as her 'secure base'. Through tuning in to her wishes and offering hours of commitment and support with *activities* and with *learning*, she is now turning towards them in her own time. They needed the help of her teacher to build a scaffold of support appropriate to her developing skills and abilities. An educational psychologist has helped to clarify Paula's individual learning journey. These are now being built through the carer's support and arose from interest-based activities as a ripple affect. Paula's overall self-esteem has gradually improved and she has great pride in her learning progress.

STEVEN, AGED 6

Vulnerabilities and adversities

Steven and his younger sister, Alison, 4 years, live with their maternal grandparents, who are in their early 60s. Their early lives have been full of a complex mixture of adversities, including the witnessing of frequent marital violence between their birth parents, and the often bizarre behaviour of their mother, who has a bipolar disorder resulting in prolonged periods of emotional unavailability to the children. Their grandfather, a consistent figure throughout their lives, is awaiting a triple bypass operation and their grandmother has recently spent several months in hospital for a serious operation on her leg.

Steven found the separation from his grandparents to start school a significant stress and his behaviour was so challenging that he was excluded in the middle of his first year. Both children were briefly accommodated in foster care with dramatic results. Neither child settled at all and they were both extremely distressed and were desperate to return to their grandfather, at that time the sole carer. The children's mother lives nearby and her mental health still fluctuates. Their father has left the area, stating that he wants nothing more to do with either child. The grandparents are very warm with both children and committed to caring for them.

Interventions

SECURE BASE

Of primary importance is the reassurance to the children of the continued availability of their grandparents. The *purpose* and hence the *shape* of contact with their mother needed to be clarified. She has agreed not to visit the grandparents' house and has some awareness that her behaviour has upset the children.

Both children appear to be attached to her, Alison more closely than Steven. It is inevitable that the children may see her in the street but structured supervised contact once a month has been established with the following purposes:

- to reassure them of her continued interest and concern

- to provide a setting in which information can be given about her well-being and whereabouts (she is due to enter a support hostel in a nearby town)

- to give the children permission to be with their grandparents and to make progress.

EDUCATION

The choice of appropriate schooling for Steven has been a vital intervention such was the disastrous nature of his first year in the local primary school. A school has been found in an adjoining town where the staff have considerable experience of working with children with a wide range of developmental problems and behavioural difficulties. They were well prepared for his admission as a whole staff group and have been able to settle him into a routine and reduce his difficult behaviour. He is now taking great pride in his ability to control himself at meal and break times without adult support.

Steven's taxi driver has become an important person as well as his class teacher. His grandparents keep regular links with the school and continue to help him with out-of-school activities which support his basic learning. Previously undetected learning difficulties have been isolated now that his behaviour has settled and learning programmes have been constructed with grandparents to shape learning tasks.

FRIENDSHIPS

The mentor gently reminds Steven when he gets into difficulty with the other children and recently he has made a friend in the team who now joins him and his mentor for the practice sessions. Steven is now very proud of his developing memory for details of his favourite team. He is collecting team memorabilia in a special book of which he is very proud.

TALENTS AND INTERESTS

Steven has a passion for football although his physical coordination is poor. A mentor has been found, a young man who is part of a local football club, who plans a career in teaching physical education. Steven sees him twice a week – once as part of a local group of children playing football and once on his own to practise. Steven's coordination is gradually improving as a result of the practice sessions and he recently scored a legitimate goal.

Messages

The two key positive interventions of finding the right school and selecting a mentor have resulted in ripple benefits for Steven.

1. He is learning about self control: his mentor helps him with ways of controlling his frustration and, through agreed signals between them, helps him to hold back from action which will alienate his team mates.

2. Memory and concentration: Steven's passion for the game is extending to the collection of pictures, league tables, goal averages, etc. such is his interest that he is learning to concentrate for longer periods. This is having a pay-off in habits of concentration at school. His reading and writing are both progressing.

3. Coordination: Steven is more aware of his body and beginning to reduce his frustration at his previous clumsiness through the repeated practice of skilled manoeuvres.

4. Skills of friendship and reciprocity: basic empathy is now being encouraged through the mentor's skilful support of Steven through fairness and turn-taking with his friend from the team.

Moral Reasoning Stages

The most famous example used to assess moral reasoning is that of Kohlberg (1969, p.379).

> In Europe, a woman was near death from a very bad disease, a special kind of cancer. There was one drug that the doctors thought might save her. It was a form of radium that a druggist in the same town had recently discovered. The drug was expensive to make, but the druggist was charging ten times what the drug cost him to make. He paid $200 for the radium and charged $2000 for a small dose of the drug. The sick woman's husband, Heinz, went to everyone he knew to borrow the money, but he could only get together about $1000, which was half of what it cost. He told the druggist that his wife was dying, and asked him to sell it cheaper or let him pay later. But the druggist said, 'No, I discovered the drug and I'm going to make money from it.' Heinz got desperate and broke into the man's store to steal the drug for his wife.
>
> Should the husband have done that? Was it right or wrong?

It is the reasons given for the answer that were more interesting to Kohlberg than the actual answer. Table A.1 shows the stages of reasoning he found. In summary the reasons given fall into one of three broad categories (Steinberg 1993): preconventional, conventional or postconventional.

Preconventional level

Typical of younger children, up to the age of about 9, this level of reasoning focuses on rewards and punishments. There is no reference to societal rules or conventions. Justifications for actions are based upon meeting one's own interests and letting others do the same. Examples of responses at this stage (from Steinberg 1993) would be that it would be right to steal the drug 'because people would have been angry with him if he let his wife die' or that he would be wrong to because he would be put in prison.

Conventional level

This level is demonstrated from middle childhood and into adolescence and often beyond into adulthood. The focus here is more upon how others, especially significant others, will judge you. There is appeal to social rules that should be upheld. It is considered important to be a 'good' person and to demonstrate trust, loyalty, respect and gratitude. 'One behaves properly because, in so doing, one receives the approval of others and helps maintain social order.' Examples of responses here would be that he should not steal because it is against the law, or that he should steal because it is what is expected of a good husband.

Postconventional or principled level

The subject of much debate and not widely found in empirical studies, this level represents reasoning that is based upon principles of justice, fairness, the sanctity of human life and so on. It is argued to be appropriate to break the law on occasions where the law violates a fundamental principle. An example of a response would be that Heinz should not steal the drug because by doing so he violates a principle that everyone has the right to pursue a livelihood. Another example would be that he should steal because preserving life is more important than the right to make a living.

Table A.1 Kohlberg's stages of moral development

Level 1: **Preconventional** morality	
Stage 1: Punishment-and-obedience orientation	What is right is whatever others permit; what is wrong is what others punish. There is no conception of rules. The seriousness of a violation depends on the magnitude of the consequence.
Stage 2: Individualism and instrumental orientation	Rules are followed only when it is in the child's immediate interest. Right is what gains rewards or when there is an equal exchange ('you scratch my back and I'll scratch yours').
Level 2: **Conventional** morality	
Stage 3: Mutual interpersonal expectations, relationships, and conformity	'Being good' means living up to other people's expectations, having good intentions, and showing concern about others. Trust, loyalty, respect and gratitude are valued.
Stage 4: Social system and conscience	'Right' is a matter of fulfilling the actual duties to which you have agreed. Social rules and conventions are upheld except where they conflict with other social duties. Contributing to society is 'good'.
Level 3: **Postconventional** morality	
Stage 5: Social contract or utility and individual rights	People hold a variety of values and opinions, and while rules are relative to the group these should be upheld because they are part of the social contract. Rules that are imposed are unjust and can be challenged. Some values, such as life and liberty, are non-relative and must be upheld regardless of majority opinion.
Stage 6: Universal ethical principles	Self-chosen ethical principles determine what is right. In a conflict between law and such principles, it is right to follow one's conscience. The principles are abstract moral guidelines organized into a coherent value system.

Source: Reproduced with permission from Schaffer 1996, p.295

Bibliography

Ainsworth, M. D. S., Blehar, M., Walters, E. and Walls, S. (1978) *Patterns of Attachment.* Hillsdale, NJ: Erlbaum.

Benson, P. L. (1997) *All Kids are our Kids: What Communities Must Do to Raise Caring and Responsible Children and Adolescents.* San Francisco, CA: Jossey-Bass.

Bernard, B. (1991) *Fostering Resiliency in Kids: Protective Factors in the Family, School and Community.* Portland, OR: Northwest Regional Education Laboratory.

Bigelow, B. J. and La Gaipa, J. J. (1980) 'The development of friendship values and choice.' In H. C. Foot, A. J. Chapman and J. R. Smith (eds) *Friendships and Social Relations in Children.* Chichester: Wiley.

Bronfenbrenner, U. (1989) 'Ecological systems theory.' *Annals of Child Development 6*, 187–249.

Brooks, R. B. (1994) 'Children at risk: fostering resilience and hope.' *American Journal of Orthopsychiatry 64*, 4, 545–553.

Bryant, B. K. (1982) 'An index of empathy for children and adolescents.' *Child Development 53*, 413–425.

Buss, A. H. and Plomin, R. A. (1984) *Temperament Theory of Personality Development.* New York: Wiley-Interscience.

Chess, S. and Thomas, A. (1977) 'Temperamental individuality from childhood to adolescence.' *Journal of Child Psychiatry 16*, 218–226.

Coie, J. D. and Dodge, K. A. (1983) 'Continuities and changes in children's social status: a five year longitudinal study.' *Merrill-Palmer Quarterly 29*, 261–282.

Coie, J. D. and Dodge, K. A. (1998) 'Aggression and antisocial behavior.' In W. Damon and N. Eisenberg (eds) *Handbook of Child Psychology: Vol. 3. Social, Emotional, and Personality Development.* New York: Wiley.

Coopersmith, S. (1997) *Coopersmith Self-Esteem Inventories.* Palo Alto, CA: Consulting Psychologists Press.

Crouch, J. L. and Milner, J. S. (1993) 'Effects of child neglect upon children.' *Criminal Justice and Behaviour 20*, 1, 49–65.

Daniel, B. M., Wassell, S. and Gilligan, R. (1999) *Child Development for Child Care and Protection Workers*. London: Jessica Kingsley.

Dodge, K. A., Pettit, G. S., McClaskey, C. L. and Brown, M. M. (1986) 'Social competence in children.' *Monographs of the Society for Research in Child Development 51*, 2.

Dowling, E. and Osborne, E. (1985) *The Family and the School: A Joint Approach to Problems with Children*. London: Routledge.

Downes, C. (1992) *Separation Revisited: Adolescents in Foster Family Care*. Aldershot: Ashgate.

Dunn, J. (1993) *Young Children's Close Relationships: Beyond Attachment*. London: Sage.

Dunn, J. and Kendrick, C. (1982) *Siblings: Love, Envy and Understanding*. Oxford: Basil Blackwell.

Eisenberg, N., Miller, P. A., McNally, S. and Shea, C. (1991) 'Prosocial development in adolescence: a longitudinal study.' *Developmental Psychology 27*, 5, 849–857.

Fahlberg, V. I. (1991) *A Child's Journey through Placement*. London: British Agencies for Adoption and Fostering.

Feeney, J. and Noller, P. (1996) *Adult Attachment*. Thousand Oaks, CA: Sage.

Fergusson, D. M. and Lynskey, M. T. (1996) 'Adolescent resiliency to family adversity.' *Journal of Child Psychology and Psychiatry 37*, 3, 281–292.

Feschbach, N. D. (1984) 'Empathy, empathy training and the regulation of aggression in elementary school children.' In R. M. Kaplan, V. J. Konecni and R. W. Novaco (eds) *Aggression in Children and Youth*. The Hague: Martinus Nijhoff.

Fonagy, P., Steele, M., Steele, H., Higgitt, A. and Target, M. (1994) The Emanuel Miller Memorial Lecture 1992: 'The theory and practice of resilience.' *Journal of Child Psychology and Psychiatry 35*, 2, 231–257.

Foot, H. C., Morgan, M. J. and Shute, R. H. (1990) 'Children's helping relationships: an overview.' In H. C. Foot, M. J. Morgan and R. H. Shute (eds) *Children Helping Children*. Chichester: Wiley.

Fox, N. A., Kimmerly, N. L. and Schafer, W. D. (1991) 'Attachment to mother/attachment to father: a meta-analysis.' *Child Development 62*, 210–225.

Garbarino, J., Dubrow, N., Kosteleny, K. and Pardo, C. (1992) *Children in Danger: Coping with the Consequences of Community Violence*. San Francisco, CA: Jossey-Bass.

Gilligan, R. (1997) 'Beyond permanence? The importance of resilience in child placement practice and planning.' *Adoption and Fostering 21*, 1, 12–20.

Gilligan, R. (1998) 'The importance of schools and teachers in child welfare.' *Child and Family Social Work 3*, 1, 13–26.

Gilligan, R. (1999) 'Children's own social networks and network members: key resources in helping children at risk.' In M. Hill (ed) *Effective Ways of Working with Children and their Families*. London: Jessica Kingsley.

Goldstein, A. P. (1999) *The Prepare Curriculum: Teaching Prosocial Competencies*. Champaign, IL: Research Press.

Golombok, S. and Fivush, R. (1994) *Gender Development.* Cambridge: Cambridge University Press.

Grotberg, E. (1997) 'The international resilience project.' In M. John (ed) *A Charge against Society: The Child's Right to Protection.* London: Jessica Kingsley.

Harris, P. L., Olthof, T., Meerum Terwogt, M. and Hardman, C. E. (1987) 'Children's knowledge of situations that provoke emotion.' *International Journal of Behavioural Development 10*, 319–343.

Harter, S. (1985) *The Self-Perception Profile for Children.* Denver, CO: University of Denver.

Hartup, W. W. (1992) 'Friendships and their developmental significance.' In H. McGurk (ed) *Childhood Social Development: Contemporary Perspectives.* Hove: Erlbaum.

Holmes, J. (1993) 'Attachment theory: a biological basis for psychotherapy.' *British Journal of Psychiatry 163*, 430–438.

Howe, D. (1995) *Attachment Theory for Social Work Practice.* London: Macmillan.

Howe, D., Brandon, M., Hinings, D. and Schofield, G. (1999) *Attachment Theory, Child Maltreatment and Family Support.* London: Macmillan.

Jackson, S. (1995) 'Education in care: not somebody else's problem.' *Professional Social Work,* November, 12–13.

Kohlberg, L. (1969) 'Stages and sequence: the cognitive-developmental approach to socialization.' In D. A. Goslin (ed) *Handbook of Socialization Theory and Research.* Chicago: Rand McNally.

Kreidler, W. J. (1984) *Creative Conflict Resolution.* Glenview, IL: London: Scott, Foresman.

Luthar, S. S. (1991) 'Vulnerability and resilience: a study of high-risk adolescents.' *Child Development 62*, 600–612.

McClellan, D. E. and Katz, L. G. (1992) 'Assessing the social development of young children: a checklist of social attributes.' *Dimensions of Early Childhood 21*, 1, 9–10.

Maccoby, E. E. and Jacklin, C. N. (1987) 'Gender segregation in children.' In H. W. Reese (ed) *Advances in Child Development and Behaviour 20.* New York: Academic Press.

Main, M. and Weston, D. R. (1981) 'The quality of the toddler's relationship to mother and to father: related to conflict behaviour and the readiness to establish new relationships.' *Child Development 52*, 932–940.

Malik, N. M. and Furman, W. (1993) 'Practitioner review: problems in childrens's peer relations: what can the clinician do?' *Journal of Child Psychology 34*, 8, 1303–1326.

Masten, A. (1994) 'Resilience in individual development.' In M. C. Wang and E. W. Gordon (eds) *Educational Resilience in Inner-City America.* Hillsdale, NJ: Erlbaum.

Masten, A. S. and Coatsworth, J. D. (1998) 'The development of competence in favorable and unfavorable environments.' *American Psychologist 53*, 2, 205–220.

Masten, A. S., Best, K. M. and Garmezy, N. (1990) 'Resilience and development: contributions from the study of children who overcome adversity.' *Development and Psychopathology 2*, 425–444.

Meadows, S. (1986) *Understanding Child Development.* London: Routledge.

Parker, R., Ward, H., Jackson, S., Aldgate, J. and Wedge, P. (1991) *Looking after Children: Assessing Outcomes in Child Care.* London: HMSO.

Petersen, C. and Seligman, M. E. P. (1985) 'The learned helplessness model of depression: current status of theory and research.' In E. Beckham (ed) *Handbook of Depression: Treatment, Assessment and Research.* Homewood, IL: Dorsey Press.

Peterson, L. and Gannoni, A. (1992) *Manual for Social Skills Training in Young People with Parent and Teacher Programmes.* Melbourne: Australian Council for Educational Research; available in UK from NFER-Nelson (01236 437457).

Piaget, J. (1952) *The Origins of Intelligence in Children.* New York: International Universities Press.

Promoting Social Competence (1999) University of Dundee and the Scottish Executive. http://www.dundee.ac.uk/psychology/prosoc.htm.

Quinton, D., Pickles, A., Maughan, B. and Rutter, M. (1993) 'Partners, peers and pathways: assortative pairing and continuities in conduct disorder.' *Development and Psychopathology 5,* 763–783.

Raundalen, M. (1991) *Care and Courage.* Sweden: Rädda Barnen.

Rutter, M. (1985) 'Resilience in the face of adversity: protective factors and resistance to psychiatric disorder.' *British Journal of Psychiatry 147,* 598–611.

Rutter, M. (1991) 'Pathways from childhood to adult life: the role of schooling.' *Pastoral Care,* September, 3–10.

Rutter, M. and Rutter, M. (1993) *Developing Minds: Challenge and Continuity across the Life Span.* Harmondsworth: Penguin.

Santrok, J. W. (1994) *Child Development.* Madison, WI and Dubuque, IA: W. C. B. Brown and Benchmark.

Schaffer, H. R. (1996) *Social Development.* Oxford: Blackwell.

Schaffer, H. R. and Emerson, P. E. (1964) 'The development of social attachments in infancy.' *Monographs of the Society for Research in Child Development 29,* 3, (whole no. 94)

Scottish Office (1999) *Social Inclusion: Opening the Door to a Better Scotland – Strategy.* Edinburgh: The Scottish Office.

Smith, C. and Carlson, B. E. (1997) 'Stress, coping, and resilience in children and youth.' *Social Service Review 71,* 2, 231–256.

Smith, P. K. and Cowie, H. (1991) *Understanding Children's Development.* Oxford: Blackwell.

Spence, S. H. (1995) *Social Skills Training: Enhancing Social Competence with Children and Adolescents.* Windsor: NFER-Nelson.

Steinberg, L. (1993) *Adolescence.* New York: McGraw-Hill.

Stewart, D. W. and Shamdasani, P. N. (1990) *Focus Groups: Theory and Practice.* London: Sage.

Terwogt, M. M. and Stegge, H. (1998) 'Children's perspective on the emotional process.' In A. Campbell and S. Mincer (eds) *The Social Child.* Hove: Psychology Press.

Thompson, R. A. (1995) *Preventing Child Maltreatment through Social Support.* Thousand Oaks, CA: Sage.

Vygotsky, L. S. (1962) *Thought and Language.* Cambridge, MA: MIT Press.

Werner, E. (1990) 'Protective factors and individual resilience.' In S. Meisels and J. Shonkoff (eds) *Handbook of Early Childhood Intervention*. Cambridge: Cambridge University Press.

Werner, E. E. and Smith, R. S. (1992) *Overcoming the Odds: High Risk Children from Birth to Adulthood*. Ithaca, NY: Cornell University Press.

Zahn-Waxler, C., Radke-Yarrow, M. and King, R. A. (1979) 'Child-rearing and children's prosocial initiations towards victims of distress.' *Child Development 50*, 319–330.

Subject Index

Author Index